NON-BOURGEOIS
THEOLOGY

NON-BOURGEOIS THEOLOGY

AN AFRICAN EXPERIENCE OF JESUS

Joseph G. Donders

ORBIS BOOKS
Maryknoll, New York 10545

The Catholic Foreign Mission Society of America (Maryknoll) recruits and trains people for overseas missionary service. Through Orbis Books Maryknoll aims to foster the international dialogue that is essential to mission. The books published, however, reflect the opinions of their authors and are not meant to represent the official position of the Society.

Copyright © 1985 by Joseph G. Donders

Published by Orbis Books, Maryknoll, NY 10545

Manuscript editor: Mary Heffron

Library of Congress Cataloging in Publication Data

Donders, Joseph G.
  Non-bourgeois theology.

    1. Theology, Doctrinal—Africa, Sub-Saharan—History—
20th century.   2. Africa, Sub-Saharan—Religious life and
customs.   3. Catholic Church—Africa, Sub-Saharan—History
—20th century.   4. Africa, Sub-Saharan—Church history.
I. Title.
BR1430.D66   1985   230′.0967   84-16677
ISBN 0-88344-352-X (pbk.)

Contents

Preface

With some exceptions all the chapters of this book were first published in article form in Dutch periodicals (*Tijdschrift voor Theologie; De Bazuin; Wereld en Zending; Memisa Nieuws; Hervormd Nederland;* and *Bijeen*). Some were originally written for *The Tablet* and the British mission journal *Now*. Others, delivered during the Salzburger Hochschulwochen of 1980, were published first in German under the title "Einfluss der Christlichen Kultur auf das Afrikanische Menschenbild" in *Kultur als christlicher Auftrag heute* (Ed. Ansgar Paus, Verlag Butzon and Bercker, Kevelaer, 1981). They have been translated, rewritten, and updated for this book. Some chapters never have been published.

An attempt has been made to avoid all unnecessary footnotes and "elitist" theological language. The book tries to capture the symbolism, the mood, the experience, the dreams, and the vision of people as they are. As will become obvious to the reader, those people are mainly Christians in their rapidly urbanizing East African environment. They often go unnamed as their experiences seemed to be more than mere individual perceptions.

The author is grateful to the hundreds and hundreds of people who made this book possible. The final redaction and interpretation is solely the author's responsibility.

Introduction

The increasing acceptance of Jesus Christ in Africa is one of the most astonishing religious phenomena of our times. Sometimes this success is contrasted with the slow note of Christian growth in Muslim or Asian areas. It is often said that Christianity is not successful when it meets other organized religions and that its success in Africa was due to the continent's unorganized religious situation. It is, however, not true that religion is not organized in Africa; it is tightly organized.

The real reasons for the growth of Christianity in Africa are different. They are especially important at this time, when Christianity in the West seems to be in a crisis and when many Western Christians are looking for a more satisfactory, non-bourgeois theology. African Christianity, the developing African Christian culture, is going to influence the rest of Christianity, as Walbert Bühlmann points out.[1]

In 1980 there were 203 million Christians in Africa. The number is growing at a rate of 4 percent a year. In certain countries of Africa the growth rate is as high as 10 percent a year. The figures suggest that Christians in Africa are increasing by 6,200,000 a year. By the year 2000 there will be about 350 million Christians in Africa, more Christians than on any other continent.

It is as if Jesus Christ really comes home in Africa, comes into his own. The poetic and mystical Jesuit scholar Pierre Teilhard de Chardin would have been delighted by this development. He was convinced that the first human home was in Africa. This conjecture seems to have been proved by the recent discoveries of the Leakey family at the shores of Lake Turkana (formerly Lake Rudolf) in Kenya. There in East Africa humankind formed its first culture in relation to surrounding nature. There humanity thought out its first theologies and its first survival patterns. Ac-

1

cording to Teilhard, humanity went out from there to spread over the earth, adapting and developing over millions of years to all kind of environments. Now, after having wandered all over the globe, those emigrants are returning to their original home, to their own roots, to their original sources, to the fountain of human life.

FIRST CONTACT

The first Christian missionaries to Africa in modern times did not think in Teilhardian terms. They came to convert. They came to save.

The first Christian missionaries in East Africa were two Germans, Krapf and Rebmann. They opened their first church in 1846 about twenty kilometers from Mombasa. They had learned to speak the local language, and they invited the local population to the church. Fifteen Warabai came. When the service (probably a classic Lutheran church service) was over, Krapf and Rebmann rushed to the entrance of the building to hear the first reactions of the people. Those reactions were far from enthusiastic. When asked whether they would come again the next Sunday, the firm answer was No. When asked why not, the people answered that they were accustomed to worshipping in another way. A bullock should have been slaughtered; there should have been rice and plenty to eat and to drink. There should have been drumming, dancing, and singing. Krapf and Rebmann told the people that they were speaking like that because they were sinners. The people asked what it meant to be a sinner. When Krapf explained the notion, the Warabai asked him who had been slandering them. When Rebmann explained that God had sent his only Son to show them his love, they said that they did not need that Son to know that God loved them. They knew about that love because God had given them their lives; God gave them their children, the sun and the moon, the rain and the harvest, their clothing and their beer. Krapf and Rebmann understood that they had not been understood.

The Warabai had not contradicted the missionaries, but they had interpreted everything they had been told from their own perspective. The Warabai amended and corrected the missionaries' message from the very beginning. The African confrontation with Christian culture had begun. Pope John Paul II's experience was similar to that of those first missionaries when he visited Africa almost 150 years later. During the offertory of a Mass the pope celebrated in Nairobi, live animals, fruits, beer, and sugar-cane were brought to the altar. Two goats, tied to the altar, were bleating all during Mass. Drums were beaten, and people danced.

HUMAN LIFE

The Christian missionaries studied African customs from the very beginning. Usually those studies were approached in a negative way. The customs studied would appear later in the catechisms as forbidden superstitions. Africans were not allowed to thank God for the reappearance of the sun in the morning by spitting in its direction. They were not allowed to make a libation of a few drops of their drink to honor the ancestors; they were not allowed to have their children circumcised. It would be some time before less negative studies would be done.

The pioneer in a new type of study was a Belgian, a Flemish Franciscan, Father Placide Tempels. In 1943 he published a revolutionary book, *Bantu Philosophy*, which became a classic in its field.[2] The most remarkable thing about the book was not so much the content, but rather that a missionary suggested that the Bantu *Weltanschauung* might be an ordered, explanatory, and scientific philosophical system.

Bantu Philosophy has been criticized, but it was the ancestor of many subsequent studies published on African philosophy, both in English and in French. Some have accused the book of being colonialistic (it was written in the early 1940s in order to help the Belgian administration in the Congo understand and rule the Congolese). Others have accused the book of mystifying African philosophy (its sources are folk traditions, which in the West would never have been accepted as sources of philosophy). Notwithstanding this sometimes justifiable criticism, the main theme of the book remains valid.

African philosophy is concerned with life, with life-power. This is of course an oversimplification, just as it is an oversimplification to say that Hindu philosophy is concerned with an escape from this world and a return to Nirvana, that Chinese philosophy is interested in internal harmony (*tao*), and that Western philosophy concerns itself with the composition of the things in this world. It is nevertheless true to say that the primary African philosophical interest is life, the gift God gave and continues to give to this world.

Tempels' disciple, the Ruandese priest-philosopher Alexis Kagame, corrected his master.[3] Through a linguistic analysis of the Bantu languages he concluded that the focus of African philosophy is not simply life but *human* life. Kagame pointed out that in Bantu philosophy human life plays a role different from its role in the philosophy of Aristotle. Whereas in Aristotle's philosophy one concept (such as "substance") can be applied to different realities (things, plants, animals, human beings, and God), this possibility does not exist in the Bantu languages. In fact Bantu languages allow only three categories of reality, and each is totally different from the others.

First, there is God, who is apart from all the rest. Next, there is the category of human beings with their intelligence. In the third category are all other things, alive or not, that are in their turn totally different from human beings and that, because they have no intelligence, are defined as being "not human." For the human being, *human life* is the all-important, the central reality. Practically all African political leaders have come to this same conclusion, though they differ in their practical policies. Kaunda of Zambia, Nyerere of Tanzania, Obote of Uganda, and Nkrumah of Ghana—all based their philosophy on this type of anthropocentric vision.

Kenyatta, of Kenya, stressed the same idea in a more playful way. He was of the opinion that the core of African culture consists in the dance—not the dance around something or someone, but the dance of the dancing people. According to him the center of African culture and of African society is the celebration of human life, and that is what the dance is. In his study *Philosophie de l'Afrique noire*, Henri Maurier summarizes all this is a more academic way:

> In Africa the human being is the center of experience and philosophy, and not the cosmos, the things, being, the One,

or the future. The African anthropocentrism is communitarian. The African starts his reflection: "We, I together with. . . ."[4]

Human life has always been of interest to the philosophers of the Western tradition. We have only to recall the interest in ethical issues of thinkers like Socrates, Plato, and Aristotle. And yet was it not Aristotle who remarked about his own philosophical school that its first question in Milete had been: What are things made of? That first question showed that Greek philosophers worked from the very beginning with a priority list different from that of their African counterparts.

During his visits to Africa, Pope John Paul II gave many speeches and addresses. In those talks he expressed one of the leading ideas of his philosophy and of Western philosophy. The pope formulated that philosophy in his phenomenological study *The Acting Person*.[5] In that book he criticizes the Cartesian idea "I am because I think." He shows in his analysis that it is not only thinking, it is not only rationality, that makes a person human. He proves that there is more to the human personality than intellect. But he remains faithful to the individualistic approach to the human being that is so typical of Descartes and of practically the whole of Western philosophy. Only in the last chapter of his book does he express any doubt about the validity of his analysis.

The question may arise, however, whether the experience of "acting together with others" was not the fundamental experience, and if so, whether the conception of the community and intersubjective relations should not be presupposed in any discussion on the acting person.[6]

He then answers his own question by arguing that, if we started from the communitarian aspect, transcendental human individuality with all its personal rights would perhaps not be disclosed.

This point of view might be understandable within the philosophical and political context from which Karol Wojtyla comes. But when Pope John Paul II communicated to his African listeners this point of view he must have caused wonderment. In Nairobi he told the African diplomatic corps:

If we want to understand the situation in Africa, its past and its future, we must start from the truth of the African person, the truth of every African in his or her concrete and historical setting. . . . The truth about the African individual must be seen first and foremost in his or her dignity as a human person.[7]

When he addressed an enormous crowd in Uhuru Park in the same city the pope said (speaking of the political challenge facing each Christian): "If the Christian finds injustice or anything that militates against love, peace and unity in society, he or she must ask: 'Where have I fallen short? What have I done wrong? What did I fail to do, that the truth of my vocation called me to do? Did I sin by omission?'"[8]

All this is valid. In Africa persons understand their personal dignity; nevertheless in the African view a person is seen first and foremost as a social being, a community member, a participant in the common human life. The Ghanaian scholar John S. Pobee noted in his book *Toward an African Theology*: "Sociologists have long pointed out that while Descartes philosophized *cogito ergo sum*, the Akan society would rather argue *cognatus ergo sum*, 'I belong by blood relationship, therefore I am.' "[9] It was strange and significant that the pope overlooked the African view completely.

In the context of the above it becomes obvious that any consideration of the influence of Western Christian culture in Africa is a delicate issue. Our speaking about Africa already involves unforgivable oversimplifications. In speaking about Christian culture we are also guilty of inexcusable generalizations. However, the main difficulty is that what we call Christian culture seems to change its significance and its meaning when put in the African context. Even the most simple terms—person, time, life, family, community, health, sickness, spirit, environment, God, and grace—become equivocal. They mean one thing and yet they also mean something different.

To illustrate this point I refer once more to the visit to Africa of that Western pilgrim Pope John Paul II. When the pope greeted the crowd who had come to welcome him at Jomo Kenyatta Airport, he said what was apparently a simple thing. "I greet you coming from the mountains and the plains, from the rivers and the valleys, from the lakes and the ocean.'' That is what he said. Some days later the chairman of the Catholic Lay Council in Kenya explained these words over the radio. He told his listeners that the pope had invoked the ancestors, even the old gods inhabiting the mountain tops, the rivers, and the lakes. In fact the pope—without knowing what he was doing—had spoken an African formula used to invoke those spirits and forces.

Several times the pope referred to the family as to the "domestic'' church and the "domestic sanctuary,'' without realizing how this would be interpreted by his hearers. That interpretation too was aired over local radio stations. The commentator reminded his listeners that in most African traditional societies the patriarch or matriarch in the family functioned as a priest, and he added that in the Catholic priesthood, as imported from Western Europe, the priest is someone from outside the family. He said that this was one of the reasons that parents in Africa were losing their authority, and then, referring to the pope's words, he suggested that all this was going to change. In a few years' time every extended family would have its priest—an idea, I am sure, that never occurred to the pope. He would probably be the first to resist such a development.

The paradoxical situation in which Christian culture finds itself in Africa is of course known to the Africans. African literature is full of the description, sometimes bitter, sometimes humorous, sometimes full of frustration, of this schizophrenic situation. Michael Imoukhuede, a young Nigerian author, wrote:

> Here we stand,
> confused children,
> umbilically connected to two civilizations,
> we find our position uneasy,
> we would like something to happen,
> so that we would be pushed either
> to this or to that side,
> we are now standing in the half-dark,
> looking for a hand that will help us,
> but we don't find it,
> I am tired, O God, I am tired,

tired of being suspended halfway,
but where shall we go?

Other Africans do not see the situation in so somber a way. Some say candidly that they think they have an advantage over the Westerner. "We are at home in two cultures," they say, "and you only in one." Whatever truth or untruth there may be in that statement, it is obvious that a uniquely African response to Christianity is developing. In that response the main elements of Christianity seem to find a typical African interpretation—an interpretation that is different from the Western one, whether it be the European, the North American, or the South American one. This development also seems to be non-bourgeois.

Formal studies of this development need to be undertaken by those, obviously, who experience the confrontation, dialogue, and growth from within themselves and their communities. A number of people already are working on these studies. For this we should be thankful to God, because the African contribution toward solving the world's existential problems is needed, and it will doubtless be fruitful.

1

The Extended African God-Experience

In 1975 a conference was held at the Nigerian university-town of Jos. The theme of the conference was "Christianity in Postcolonial Africa."[1] Theologians from all over Africa attended the conference together with quite a few European theologians. The Europeans were surprised when they heard the ideas of their African colleagues. Samuel Kibicho, a Kenyan who is chairperson of the Department of Religious Studies at the University of Nairobi and is known for his studies of the religious experiences of his people, the Gikuyu, stated that Western missionaries had not correctly translated the African names for God. According to Kibicho their translations had diminished, devaluated, reduced, and devitalized those names. He added that the real depth and height of the African names for God could not really be translated into Western theological terminology. To illustrate his point Kibicho added, provocatively, that he was not surprised that theologians in the West had been able to speak about the death of God some years ago. God had become so small and so human in the West that his death was easily feasible. Even the use of the word *his* was an indication of the smallness of the Western God. According to Kibicho it would be impossible to think of the death of God in a Gikuyu religious context. The Gikuyu experience of God is too wide, too great, too infinite, and too life-giving to allow for such a possibility. If God were dead, humanity would have died too. No wonder that some European theologians were provoked and even irritated.

During the first Pan-African Congress of Third World Theologians (Accra, Ghana, December 1977), a theologian from Bechuana recalled the discussion at Jos. In his address entitled "Where Are We in African Theology?" he too affirmed that African Christians can offer to Western believers an experience of the divine deeper, higher, more penetrating and all-pervading than the experience to which Western Christians have been accustomed. Referring to this difference of experience he added: "That is the reason that we Africans always experience difficulties with our non-African brothers and sisters at ecumenical meetings."[2]

THE HUNCHBACK-MAKER

When one tries to translate the African experience of God into Western terms, the difficulty that arises can be illustrated by an incident that occurred among the Acholi people of Uganda seventy years ago. The first Italian missionaries had arrived there in 1911. Of course they needed a name for God to be able to speak about Jesus Christ, and they looked for the Acholi name that would be most similar to the biblical name for God. They thought that the best name to use would be the Acholi equivalent for the biblical word 'creator.' That is the reason that they asked the Acholi in their research: Who made you? The Acholi had no answer to that question. The missionaries then changed their question and, thinking of the bible story in which God took earth to model humanity, they asked: Who formed you? and they explained what they meant by that question. The Acholi had never heard such a story. The only divinity they could connect with the missionaries' report on someone taking earth to form a human being was Lubanga or Rubanga. This was their name for a divinity who, according to their traditional stories, broke the spines of human beings and thus gave them a new form. Rubanga was the "creator" or "former" of hunchbacks. But they did not tell the full story to the missionaries, who were very glad to have found a name for God. So it was that the whole of Acholiland began to pray in the first Christian churches to Rubanga, the hunchback-maker, the causer of spinal tuberculosis and other similar diseases, who, according to those missionaries, was also the Father of Jesus Christ.

Kibicho's observations and those of other African theologians remain hanging in mid-air as long as they do not go on to describe in more detail the African experience of God. A major difficulty is that Africa is so large—it encompasses so many different peoples and languages. Is it really possible to speak of one African experience of God? It does seem possible. Again and again one finds in the writings of African authors from all over the continent remarks such as this:

> What struck us Africans was the unity and uniformity of our assumptions. From whatever place in Africa we were coming, either geographically or ecclesiastically, whether we were Roman Catholics, Methodists, or Reformed, whether we came from the South, the East or the West, we always agreed on those assumptions.[3]

HUMAN LIFE AND GOD

It is in the relationship between human life and God that all Africans seem to experience God in a way different from Westerners. That difference has to do with the African idea of God as creator. In most African traditional stories it is not God who forms human bodies—that part of creation is left to a lesser divinity. But it is God who gives humanity its life.

In the Western interpretation of our common beginning, God also gives life. God blew breath into the human being after having formed its shape out of earth. After that God seems to have left humanity alone, according to the biblical report. God had given human beings their life and they were supposed to go it alone after that, though they remained dependent on God, who preserved them.

The African interpretation differs from this. Humanity remains dependent on God in a different way. God continues, so to speak, to blow life into human beings all the time. Our lives constantly flow from God through our ancestors and parents, and through us, the living, that lifeline flows on to our children and the children of our children. Life continuously flows from its source—God—through the channel of our human genealogical history to us and through us on into the future. The African idea lies somewhere between the Hindu idea of emanation and the biblical creation story. The difference can best be seen by studying the African interpretation of the relationship between parents and their children. Parents do not give life to their children at one point, the moment of conception or the moment of birth; they continue to give life. *It is this idea that makes practically everything in African theology and philosophy different from the Western (or Eastern) view.*

We will come back frequently to this insight. One of the consequences of this idea is that parents really can bless their children by letting life flow to them without interruption; another consequence is that parents really can curse their children by refusing to continue to give them life. There are known cases in which fierce adult warriors literally fell dead at the moment that their mothers cursed them, lifting up their skirts and showing them those parts of their bodies through which the warriors had come into this world, saying: "These are the gates through which you came into life; they are going to be closed. Cursed be you." They slapped back their skirts and the effect was instantaneous.[4]

It is not only human life that continues to flow from God. All the other life that is necessary to keep humankind alive, the life of the plants, the animals, and the minerals (that in their "powers" live also)—it all flows continuously from God. No wonder that in this context one of the most interesting points of discussion on God in Africa revolves around the question of whether God is an ancestor or a creator.[5]

CHAIN OF LIFE

The flow of life is a necessary condition of our being able to live. But to receive life is not sufficient to live. Really to live we in our turn must pass on life. It is in the stream that one lives. If we did not pass on life we would be stagnant pools, and not really living links in the life chain. This necessary element in life makes any appreciation for celibacy practically impossible. It is in the African vision, not only abnormal not to pass on life; it is also just plain bad. It is a refusal to use God's most important gift to humankind.

Imported Christian culture explains that to give life is to give something not only physical—there is also a "spiritual" parenthood. But the problem of celibacy is not solved by this explanation, if only because spiritual life is not the same as human life. In the African vision the spiritual is only an aspect of human life.

NOT ONLY FATHER

Within this frame of reference God cannot be only a father. African children often ask: Who is my mother? when they are told that God is their father. The African child depends so long and so intimately on its mother that this question is to be expected. In the African experience of God, God is as much and as often a mother as a father.

A father loves his children in a way different from a mother. On that issue all psychologists seem to agree. The father loves his children mainly because of their performance, but a mother loves her children by the simple fact that her children are her children. Any visit to an African prison indicates that the psychologists are right. Prisoners are rarely visited by their fathers. The fathers are sometimes so ashamed of their criminal child that they even change their names. Mothers do visit their imprisoned sons and daughters. They say: "Whatever others might say—that he is a murderer, a monster or whatever—he remains my son." The two kinds of love (and they are of course not exclusive) are both necessary for a healthy growing process.

We in the West overplay God's father-role and pay insufficient attention to her mother-role. Significant insight into the mother-role God plays in the Bible has been developing only recently in the West. That insight is going to influence the whole of theology, especially, to give only one example, our idea about the possibility and eventuality of eternal punishment in hell. It is in that mother-role that God says in the Bible: Even if a mother would be able to forget about the child she is suckling at her breast, I will never forget you (see Is 49:15). And Jesus said: How often have I not longed to collect you under my wings just like a mother hen collects her chickens (see Lk 13:34; cf. Dt 32:11). That same Bible tells from the very beginning that "in the image of God he created him, male and female he created them" (Gn 1:27).

Kibicho and Setiloane hold that to the African God is neither a "he" nor a "she," but is rather an "it." They too describe God as the creator and life-giver, as father and mother. A very old African image of God is that of the *tree* of life. One of the characteristics of that symbol might be bisexuality (though that is not true of all trees).

W. Eggen, a missionary in Central African Republic, studied the name of God among the Banda people. The first missionaries in that country also had difficulty in finding a proper vernacular name for God. One of the names they found was *Ere*. It was a name found in many proverbs and sayings. The word *ere*, however, could also mean "thing," so the word was used a thousand times a day. When the Banda wanted to bless someone they said: "May Ere bless you." But when they said: "Ere is not here," they were indicating that nothing was present. The missionaries therefore made a linguistic distinction between the word *Ere* meaning "God" and *ere* meaning "thing." Eggen suggests that they were wrong to do this. The Banda speak in this way of a nonpersonal, undefinable dimension of reality comprising everything that only could be named in a neutral way—*ere*: thing, it. Thus God remains transcendent and yet near, as near as everything around them.

CONSEQUENCES

The Kenyan theologian Jesse Mugambi attempted to understand the doctrine of the Blessed Trinity in the light of the African's life-experience. Irish missionaries once tried to explain the mystery of the Blessed Trinity to him by means of a shamrock, which, according to legend, was the symbol Saint Patrick had used to explain the Trinity. Mugambi was not impressed, as the missionaries never could explain to him the origin of the stem of that leaf.

If God is alive, then God must pass on life. Without that passing on of life, life is stagnant and not real. If a young man dies without having become a father, he really dies. So God gives life. But there is always a giver and a receiver. If God gives life, there must be a bond, a life-bond, between the giver and the receiver. We Westerners would then count: one, two, three—giver, receiver, bond. An African does not count. Life is not counted.

Human beings should never be counted. If a teacher starts to count the children in the class, they will often shout: Do not count us, we are not sheep! In a traditional African context parents never give an exact answer to the question: How many children do you have? They give a vague approximative answer.

Just as God gives life as a parent to a child, so all other life is given. Did not John suggest in his Gospel that the whole of creation (or the whole of life) is given in God's Son? Did he not write that in the Son all has been created (see Jn 1:3)? This approach to christology has not been worked out yet; we are only at the beginning. Kibicho dares to suggest that we might find the beginnings of an African pneumatology in this life-idea. Is not the Spirit of God the life that is continuously flowing toward and through us?

NOT SATISFIED

In December 1976, eight hundred African church leaders came together in Nairobi for the Pan-African Christian Leadership Assembly. Those church leaders did not represent the most liberal Christian groups in Africa; they were generally fundamentalistic, evangelical, and conservative. Yet they all agreed on one point: Imported Christianity will never be able to quench the spiritual thirst of the African.

Indeed, more than eight thousand African independent churches and independent church groups have separated themselves from imported Western missionary churches. Many studies have been undertaken on this phenomenon. All kind of reasons for it have been given. It is not difficult to guess the main reason. The African does not feel at home in imported Christian church communities. But do Christians in the West feel at home in the type of Christianity they have been and still are exporting?

2

God as a Member of the Human Family

He had worked in Africa for many years. He became sick, and, as often happens in such cases, he became involved in the complicated administration of the mission society to which he belonged. He was elected to represent his province at the General Chapter. He revisited Africa to refresh his memory, to update his experience. He was disappointed by his visit. He regretted that some of the old practices had fallen away under the influence of urbanization. He deplored the disappearance of the three-year catechumenate as it had been practiced in his day. He said: "They are now baptized without any further ado. They don't even know their prayers. They are only looking for a new name. They are only looking for a new community. They don't have any faith. They hardly know anything about Jesus."

As he was complaining, you could hear singing out in the street. A group of African Christians of an independent church were dancing and singing. They were noisy, and now and then you could hear the shrill ululations of the women. They all were dressed in long white gowns on which were embroidered large red crosses. They were praying over someone who obviously wanted to be delivered of an evil spirit. The accusation, "They don't even know their prayers," sounded strange against this background of prayer. Everyone, however, knew what the visitor wanted to say.

He meant to say that Africans did not know the prayers he himself knew. Someone in the group said: "Even if what you say is true, don't the Acts of the Apostles tell us that Phillip baptized that first African, the eunuch from Ethiopia, within an hour?" I thought that he would answer something like: "Yes, but that happened to be a eunuch, no problem" or maybe "But Phillip was only a deacon" or something similar. He said something different. He said: "Don't forget, that eunuch was reading his Old Testament; he knew what he needed, he was prepared."

FROM WITHIN

This conversation took place in a presbytery in Nairobi, Kenya, in August 1980 in the midst of a group of European and Canadian missionaries. It was very revealing. It touched a sore spot, one that is indicative of all kinds of communication difficulties. The visitor, in complete good faith, not only thought that he knew what the Africans needed, but also why and how they needed it. They needed, according to him, for *their* salvation of body and soul, *his* prayers, *his* religious attitudes and motivations, and even *his* theology. It never had entered his mind that those prayers, attitudes, motivations, and theology had been developed and practiced in different times, places, and circumstances.

That Africans wanted to get a new name to start a new life, that they deemed it necessary to belong to a new community meant, according to his own words, *everything* to them and *nothing* to him. It escaped him entirely that Africans struggle in their own religious tradition and history with the same problems the Jews had struggled with in the Old Testament.

Fortunately, this type of Western missionary mentality is disappearing. However, this spiritual paternalism has not vanished completely. Jesus is still preached as he was digested (and often betrayed) in the West. He is preached as if he only came to announce his name and salvation in that name. It is often forgotten and sometimes denied that he came to share our lives to help us to solve our problems, that he came to give us a better idea about how to live those lives. Missionaries and bishops are still building parish churches and cathedrals in the Western style, sometimes even before they have a single church member. Later they are amazed and surprised that even after the people have become Christian, they do not come to the churches, but pray in the open, under the trees, as their ancestors have done from time immemorial.

The African desire to be baptized does not come from Europe or from America. It does not even come from the missionaries. That desire comes from Africans, who see something in Jesus Christ. What they see has everything to do with the solution of their problems. Those problems are not the theological questions that could be raised around the phenomenon of Jesus. The issues that interest them are life-problems: food, drink, survival, children, education, health, economics, the use of power. If Jesus wants to be truly a savior, a liberator, a helper, as an agent of salvation, he needs to function in those areas of interest. Africans who welcome Jesus into their lives believe that he will help them to deal with those issues. Because those problems are common, and because many Africans believe Jesus can help them cope with those problems, it should be no surprise that Jesus is welcomed into the African communities.

LIFE-CONTEXT

Certain aspects of missionary activity in Africa never have been described accurately in mission studies. The widely accepted idea that Africa was converted by missionaries is one of those ideas that obscure what really happened. Africa was converted and is being converted by Africans, who were and who are under the influence of the Holy Spirit. They received Jesus themselves, and they were, in their love and enthusiasm, very willing to give him to others. Jesus Christ was not accepted because the missionaries wanted it. Jesus was not welcomed because the evangelizers thought he should be welcomed in view of eternal salvation. Traditional African belief does not consider the possibility of eternal damnation, although it seems that there are some exceptions, mainly in West Africa where the African believes in the punishment of sins committed in this world. The end of time is not considered. The Africans did not look forward to heaven. In a sense they did not believe in death. Their almost exclusive interest was *this* world, the here and now of this, our human life—a life dependent on God, on the ancestors, forefathers, and foremothers, but also dependent on those still to be born. When this life was threatened, they looked around for a new organization of the life-context.

The need was not felt at the same time by everyone. Mission work proceeded slowly. Almost all the studies on the Christianization of Africa state that the first converts were the marginal cases. The mission posts were soon popular with asocial, somewhat abnormal individuals who had had difficulties within their own communities. They were the first ones to see salvation in the new community and life-context as offered by the missionaries and evangelizers. This is a story that reminds us of the story of Jesus Christ. Wasn't he surrounded by people from the margins of society?

Only when the impact of the Western way of life, with its destructive effect on the older (and perhaps indeed worn-out) communitarian patterns, was felt by all did the masses feel any need for change. Confronted with new difficulties and dangers, new threats and frustrations, but also with new possibilities, the African tried to avert the threatening disintegration by turning to Christ.

THE WARP AND THE WOOF

African converts turned to Jesus according to their own dynamics and dialectics. The acceptance of the new human being and the new God took place within their own context, their own frames of reference, and their own life-patterns. It is within their context that Jesus was received. One of the first African theologians, Harry Sawyerr from Sierra Leone, explains this in his book *Creative Evangelism*.[1]

According to Sawyerr, the African structural social pattern consists of two life-lines. First, the vertical life-line connects each human person through parents, grandparents, great-grandparents, and ancestors with God, the lasting life-giver. This vertical line also runs into the future through one's children, grandchildren, great-grandchildren, and so on. In reference to their relationship with God, the members of one clan or family stand next to the members of the other clans and families like parallel threads that run from God through history and into future life. These threads form the warp of the human social texture. But a textile with only a warp has no cohesion. You would be able to put your hand through it anywhere. For cohesion a woof is needed. Most African peoples are used to organizing that woof. The woof is the second type of life-line, a kinship that horizontally connects the families of one people or of a clan. It connects peers in a kinship of age-mates.

That kinship is born when the age-mates undergo together the initiation ritual that introduces them into adult life. The age at which this ceremony takes place differs from one people to another. It does not always take place every year; some peoples organize it every two, three, seven, or even fifteen years. The initiation can take different forms. Some groups circumcise boys and girls at about twelve years of age. Others remove some teeth; still others scar the faces of the initiates. In all cases pain is involved, and in most cases the blood of the initiates flows together on the earth. During such ceremonies all the participants of the group become brothers and sisters. In many cases the new relationship is supposed to be even stronger and more intimate than the kinship of blood brothers and blood sisters. It is a common birth into a new life. Sometimes that similarity to birth is acted out for the participants. Sawyerr uses the example of the Gikuyus in Kenya to illustrate this point. Six days after their circumcision all the boys and girls, who are kept separate up to that moment, are brought together in a large hut. An older man and a older woman are chosen as their adoptive parents. All those children are going to be born out of them. The adoptive or substituting parents go into the hut where the children are. Everyone is silent. The woman lies down on a couch. Suddenly she starts to groan and scream like a woman who is in labor. The children recognize the sounds they must have heard so often before. The husband hurries out of the house to call the midwife, who is waiting. The midwife comes; in the meantime a sheep has been slaughtered. The intestines of the sheep are cut in long, bloody strips. One end of the strip is bound to the couch on which the woman is moaning; the other end is bound around the naked children at their navels. While all the children are crying, the midwife cuts the strip that connects the laboring mother to the children, just as she would cut the umbilical cord at a real birth.

The whole group of children is thus born. The late president of Kenya, Jomo Kenyatta, wrote in his book *Facing Mount Kenya* that the children are born *as one corporate body*.[2] From then on they form "one person," *riika*, the age-mate group, and they are to live and help each other accordingly (if they remain faithful to their traditions).

The cries of the mother, the care and worry of the father, the presence of the midwife, the cutting of the umbilical cord, the whole of the ceremony call up the reality of a new birth for all the participants. They will not forget the event for the rest of their lives. The families and clans within the people are in this way horizontally interconnected.

The warp is woven through the woof. The African social structure or texture is thus strong enough to resist any attack or difficulty. No wonder that the colonial government (and the churches imported from the West) tried to undo that structure by forbidding the circumcision of girls. They also had other reasons for forbidding this, but the main reason seems to have been to break the backbone of the Gikuyu people. The structure of African society was not developed because someone introduced it from the outside. It was not introduced because someone preached it. It grew from within from a felt need; it grew because it was necessary for the survival of the people. This structure, after contact with the rest of the world, is falling away, as it does not seem to serve its purpose anymore. Other structures are needed in the new situation.

The breakup of the pattern is a serious issue for the African people. Individuals who lose their traditional bond, who are socially isolated and insulated, are often totally at a loss. They depended so much on that bond that when it disappears society itself falls away. It often means a decline in morality and ethics.

This breakup is one of the reasons for the strange behavior of many of the "elite" in Africa. In his travelogue *North of South*,[3] Shiva Naipaul describes in a penetrating (but also pessimistic) way the displaced persons one can find in the streets of an African town. Much of East African literature describes this type of person. The displaced person is one of the consequences of a transition that can only be survived by the formation of new living communities. Africa needs redemptive, even preventive, pastoral development and care.

SALVATION-LOGIC

With this kind of background, the Gikuyu listened to the first reports about Jesus. They were told that he was the Son of God, that they could be initiated into his life by baptism. He was said to have brought the fullness of human life. He died on the cross, and his blood (an important clue) dripped on the earth. Baptism meant death with him to an old life and birth into a new life. He was called savior, redeemer, all-powerful and oldest brother, the firstborn among us, and so on. Bells started ringing in their heads, and drums started sounding in their hearts—the drums used during initiation ceremonies included. The missionaries were telling them one thing, but they were hearing something else.

With all this in mind, we should note what is happening now in independent African church groups. Africans have developed, independent of catechism and Sunday school instructions, their own theologies. These theologies are independent in the sense that they have developed without interference from Rome, Geneva, or Pasadena.

Few of these numerous groups have been studied. In 1970 Barrett counted six thousand of them.[4] One of those studied was the *ahonoki* church in Kiambu, a town not far from Nairobi.[5] *Ahonoki* means the "saved ones." The members of this church consider baptism with water and the second baptism with the Holy Spirit as initiations into the life of Jesus Christ. Through their baptism they are initiated into the life he brought; they become full human beings. Their new life is their salvation. An important theological question arises. What about the possible future sins of those saved ones? Because their new life is their salvation, how can they sin after baptism? (Paul had to answer the same questions with his neophytes.)

The *ahonoki* do not believe that they cannot sin anymore. They believe they can. Their sins will be accounted for differently than the sins of those who are not "saved." God judges the sins of the *ahonoki* different from the sins of others. When *ahonoki* die they will go to God for judgment. If God, reviewing their life in the great book, comes to the conclusion that the persons in question do not deserve to enter heaven, but should go to hell, then their agemate Jesus will come forward saying: "Sorry, Father, these are my bloodbrothers, these are my bloodsisters, these are my agemates. You have to let them in!" The Father will listen. The *ahonoki* believe themselves saved and safe, because at the time of their death Jesus will play the same role any agemate would play here on earth. An agemate will support a bloodbrother or bloodsister in difficulty before a human court by paying the fine or compensating for damages.

Through baptism God relates to the human family in a new way. Before baptism, one's relationship with God ran only in a vertical line; after baptism God enters one's life through "Jesus Christ in a horizontal line. God is then part of the whole of the human structure: *Bwana Yesu karibu kwetu*, "Jesus welcome in our midst." God became in Jesus a member of the human family!

THE IMPACT

In the beginning of this chapter we noted that a missionary objected to the Africans' having their own reasons for wanting to be baptized. He complained that they did not seem to be interested in the motivations he had learned about during his own catechism classes and theological training.

Other missionaries complain in a similar but a more subtle way. Those missionaries, along with bishops and church leaders (mostly African), will say that *they* have started or are going to start "small Christian communities." They act as if the initiative comes from them. Those communities were (and are) not started from "above." They exist whether the hierarchical church likes them or not. The way in which official church leaders speak about these initiatives is often not supported by the facts. They seem to make a perhaps justifiable but rather clumsy attempt to guarantee their control. Brian Hearne, an Irish theologian in East Africa, said at the National Irish Mission Congress (Knock, 1979) that the idea of small Christian communities is in essence "a spirituality." It is not a pastoral gimmick; it is not even a pastoral strategy. It is not something church leaders are "doing" for the people.[6]

Bishop Raphael Ndingi noted at the Knock Congress that in 1973 the East African bishops began to understand that the parish structures, as they had been introduced from the West, did not suffice in the East African context and that by 1980 a change would have to take place. These parish structures, he said, only took care of the Christians in the main centers; in scores of outposts nothing happened except during the rare visits by a priest.[7] He turned official, ecclesiastical history upside down when he said that the bishops of East Africa had decided to form small Christian communities (Bishop Ndingi called them "neighborhood Christian communities") *consequent* to the grassroots initiative to form the communities. It is doubtful that all the other bishops were so glad about the formation of the communities.

3

Liturgy as a Family Feast

At the entrance to the university chapel in Nairobi is a bookshop. The woman in charge there sells books and the usual devotional items. One of the fastest selling items is a plaque with a saying printed on a green or red velvet background. The saying reads: "Jesus is the unseen guest in this house, he is the head of the family, he is with us at the table, he listens in to every conversation." The text is not new. It did not even originate in Africa, but it is a best seller there.

It is impossible to express the intensity of the sense of kinship with Jesus felt by many African Christians. Some of them talk about it almost constantly. Others place his picture in a special corner in their house. The churches are full on Sundays. But worship also takes place all over towns like Nairobi in large open-air gatherings. Processions of dancers move from one part of town to another. Some processions have developed a kind of quick-walking way of moving. Didn't Peter write to the Christians that they should hasten the end? These services last for hours and hours. Bishop Albert Yungu from Zaire wrote:

Which Christ are we going to preach in Africa? What is the most eloquent cultural element we would be able to use all over our continent? The most appropriate way seems to be to speak about our *blood relationship* with Jesus Christ. That truth is not only something that is specifically Christian (we are all brothers and sisters in Christ because of our

25

"filii in Filio"), but that blood relationship also finds a sociological and anthropological base in our African traditions as regards family—and further relationships.[1]

In a different part of Africa, Sierra Leone, Canon Harry Sawyerr noted that it is our *family-relation with Jesus* that should find expression in African liturgy. He refers to texts in the Bible that describe similar relationships with Jesus: "We are all one in Jesus"; "we are all his"; "but now in Christ Jesus you who once were far off have been brought near in the blood of Christ" (Eph. 2:13); "you are no longer strangers . . . but you are . . . of the household of God" (Eph 2:19); together with him we form a new nation, a new family (see 1 Pt 2:9).[2]

The Africans want to be taken up into that new family of God. They want to be of the family of Jesus Christ. The would like to begin with him that new, full human life. They would like to be connected with him who shed his blood on the cross when he came to the fulness of his life. It is in this way that the African reads Saint Paul: "I have been crucified with Christ; it is no longer I who live, but Christ who lives in me" (Gal 2:20). Together with Jesus we form one new family in God.

We have heard these terms in the West for years, but in Africa they have a deeper meaning. What is true of one member of the family is true of the whole family. What is true for the whole of the family is true of each of its members. In institutional terms: the church is the *extended family of Jesus* who is the head, and this family is made up of all his blood relations. Each local church is the *family of Jesus* in that place. All this could be said in a Western church. It *is* said in the official prayer of the Mass, the canon (canon 3: "Father, hear the prayers of the *family* you have gathered here before you"). Whether these concepts have much meaning where one lives within the limitations of the nuclear family remains a question.

LITURGICAL CONSEQUENCES

When a group of people shares this mentality, the liturgy that develops is quite different from the Western liturgy, even when the group remains faithful to the scheme given in the Roman missal. African Christians come together and greet each other in a sociable and pleasant way. All of them come—the grandparents, the parents, the children, and the babies. It would be considered a breach of community to organize a service only for youth or a special service for the aged ones. The celebration of Mass in a home for aged people has something peculiar about it—too much earthly past and not enough earthly future. A Mass for teenagers is strange too—too much future and not enough past. Was the old Jewish liturgy not organized in such a way that the older ones introduced the younger ones to what the celebration was about?

The Africans want to sing. Silent Masses are not popular in Africa. Melody and rhythm are essential. Gradually the whole congregation starts to move. That moving is also essential. It keeps body and spirit together. It helps us celebrate human life in all its aspects, in all its splendor, force, and vitality. It shows the celebration of the only gift God gave to this world, the only gift that really counts: our human life. The Africans celebrate that life together with children and grandchildren, with all the future promises of life that are still hidden in the wombs of the pregnant women, who join in the dance. During the "Lord have mercy, Christ have mercy" all sins and iniquities are danced away. After that, food is brought. It is put on the table because of Jesus Christ, who is the head of this family, because it is he who brings everyone together in one body and one spirit. His story is told. A sermon applies the story to the present situation. There are reactions during that sermon—approval and disapproval, weeping, laughing, and sighing. The babies who start to cry their own alleluias quickly are given the life-giving breasts of their mothers. There are prayers for special intentions. Ancestors are involved and commemorated. It is suddenly silent as the priest breaks the bread to commemorate the greatest human companion who ever lived. Some would like the bread to be a maize-, a cassava-, or a rice-pudding, and the wine a locally brewed palm-, millet-, or banana-wine. The priest prays over the wine, saying that it has been made by human hands. That prayer never refers to African human labor, but always to the work of hands in Spain, France, Cyprus, or Australia.

The kiss of peace goes through the church; it passes outside the church to all those who did not find a place inside. It passes into the village or the town. Hands are shaken, shoulders are tapped. Then the bread is eaten, *his* bread, *our* bread, so that all may form one body and one spirit. And then again everyone sings, blesses, greets. Tasks are divided and everyone leaves the church boisterously to meet friends and acquaintances outside. Slowly the church square is emptied.

In the Independent churches even all this does not satisfy the faithful. Their services sometimes last from ten in the morning until four in the afternoon. They include exorcisms, healings, speaking in tongues, prophesying, and the laying on of hands. In this way the African liturgy celebrates the God-Man Jesus, the great mediator, the priest, the bridge between God and humankind, the one we all thank for our life. He is the master of ceremonies, who, as he did in Cana, puts new wine on the table; who, as he did in Palestine, provides the bread; and who, with his flute, starts the dance. If the celebration is successful, he will not have to repeat his complaint: "We piped to you, and you did not dance" (Mt 11:17; Lk 7:32).

SWEET REVENGE

In 1977 the Undugu ("brotherhood") went to Europe. The choir was made up of twenty teenagers, boys and girls, from a parish in Nairobi. They were used to dancing and singing together with the rest of the parishioners during the liturgy. They formed a good choir.

They went to Germany, the country from which Krapf and Rebmann, the first missionaries to modern Kenya, had come. Those evangelizers had disappointed their first African visitors at a Sunday service. The Warabai worshippers had been thoroughly bored and had found the service dull and dead.

Those young Kenyans took revenge in Germany. In German churches they did what their forefathers and foremothers had not been allowed to do in their own churches. They danced and sang one of the most common village Masses from Kenya's coastal region, the Taita Mass. The enthusiasm in Germany was enormous. In the middle of large cathedrals, where normally everything is silent, where hardly anybody had ever dared to clap hands, where the old plainchant was still hanging in the high vaults, the people applauded spontaneously during the service. The applause lasted sometimes for several minutes. The boys and girls did not understand what was happening. Neither did the German churchgoers. Some of the people followed the group on their tour through Germany from Sunday to Sunday. People, after the services, said that they suddenly felt alive again. They felt the living Spirit of God moving in themselves.

The liturgy that choir brought to Germany did not much resemble the first service of the missionaries who came to Africa from that country. The African choir celebrated the same Jesus, and yet he had changed. He had another face. He was savior in a new way. Alleluia brother! Alleluia, sister!

4

God's Family

One of my first contacts with an African student was with a theology student in Kenya. We talked about the influence of Christian culture in Africa. He said that the missionaries had missed their chance. I asked him why, and he answered: "They should have used baptism much more to initiate us into one new divine community." He added, "Too often they baptized us as individuals."

According to statistics published in *Time* magazine, the average number of Africans baptized each day in 1980 was 16,550. Of those neophytes 32 percent were adults. The Muslim population of Africa also is growing (according to statistics based on the calculations of David Barrett, author of the *Christian World Encyclopedia*) by 4,750,000 annually, of which 6 percent are adults. The increase in the number of Christians in Africa is the more striking if one compares the figures of the last seventy years. In 1912 in the whole of Africa there were 1,300,000 Christians; 3,750,000 in 1924; 14,000,000 in 1949; 53,000,000 in 1962; 97,000,000 in 1969; and 203,000,000 in 1980. According to Barrett's projections Africa will count more than 350,000,000 baptized Christians by the year 2000. Africa will have the largest Christian group in the world.

Why is Christianity so attractive to Africans? There are many answers to that question—a question the Africans themselves are asking. The African theologian Gabriel Setiloane has two answers.

In the very first place I am bewitched by Jesus. In the second place I consequently rationalize my position by believing that it is not necessary to hold to every detail of Christian theology to be a believer. It is sufficient to say that Jesus Christ is the son of God, that is to say, the unique, never before occurred, and afterwards never repeated or surpassed manifestation of divinity.[1]

Edwin W. Smith, an expert in African religion, made the answering of this question his lifework. Smith (1897–1957) pointed out that God remains somewhat mysterious in the African worldview. God is considered to be far away, notwithstanding the fact that God continuously gives life to the world and to humankind. In the African vision God cannot be completely discharged from some responsibility for the sickness and death in this world. In a sense God is too often absent. How often were Ugandans heard to say during the bloody regime of General Amin and its aftermath: "God forgot our country, God is forgetting us." Misfortune is sometimes connected with a wrong done, but that is not always the case.

According to many African myths, God left this world and keeps at a distance. There are many stories explaining this distance. A typical explanation is the one the Ewe people in Ghana tell. They say that in the beginning God lived very near to the human family. There was one thing God could not stand: the smoke of their fires. When human beings increased and burned more and more fires, God got too much smoke in his eyes and went higher up in heaven. Humanity did not pay any attention and burned more and more fires, so God went higher and higher and farther and farther away. (This story might be a good start for a theology on the environment and ecology.) In other stories the reasons given for God's disappearance are the perpetual quarreling of humanity, the noise of maize grinding, and other polluting human activities.

African theologians, such as Kibicho and Mugambi, stress the point that these stories do not mean that the prevailing African idea is deistic. They do not mean that Africans believe that God does not bother at all about the universe (which from the African point of view is human life). They believe that God is involved in the affairs of humankind, and that people experience this involvement in terms of God's continuing to create, sustain, provide, nurse, heal, and save. Most of this involvement is on the concrete, physical level with special reference to human life, as John Mbiti wrote in his book *African Religions and Philosophy*.[2] Nevertheless, a distance between God and the world remains.

WELCOME

Because of the distance between God and humanity together with the belief that everything depends completely on God, the news of the appearance of God in Jesus Christ struck the Africans mightily. According to Smith, Christ was welcome. Jesus spoke to a deep-rooted and intensely felt need of the Africans, to the mystical element within the religious dynamism of the African mentality. Through him one could be connected to God in a new way. A new communion—and community—with God was possible in Jesus.

David Barrett believes that one of the main reasons Africans are so attracted to Christianity (and to Islam) is the community it offers. It is his opinion that the conversion movement at the grassroots level is due to the fact that the Africans are turning away from their local tribal religions because they see no "salvation" in those organizations anymore. They want to belong to a larger human and religious community.

This desire to belong to a community must be seen from the African point of view. It is not like belonging to a club, an association, a trade union, or similar organization. It is a deeper type of belonging. Only if we understand the depth of African community-mindedness can we understand African interest in baptism. At the same time we know that it will be difficult to satisfy that desire in a church that uses Western ideas about the individual-community relationship. In our Western churches we often speak about "Christian social teaching." That teaching is based on Christian ideas of justice, human equality, the individual dignity of the human person, and similar issues.

However, we rarely see baptism as an initiation into a new, earthly, human community. For us the formation of a community by baptism does not in fact change existing class and other structures. The rich and the poor come into those churches as rich and poor, and they remain separated. Class and other distinctions separate the faithful in the church. The only bridge over that bitter water is *charity*, which often emphasizes the differences instead of taking them away.

Another factor excludes the possibility of a Christian community. Church leaders (for instance, John Paul II) stress so much the nuclear family as the fundamental community that the more fundamental community we all belong to in God (biblically, the kingdom of God) is overlooked. The family pattern is not a generalizing pattern. Families, so to speak, stand next to each other in human society. Each is vertically connected to God the life-giver, but there is no horizontal connection between them. The lack of the horizontal relationship is obvious in our Western liturgy, where individuals and individual families sit next to each other in worship without ever knowing each other's name, without ever being introduced, sometimes without being willing to give each other the sign of peace during the celebration of their "togetherness" in Jesus Christ. Those individuals and families are there purely in their vertical life-line with God. They are vertically connected with God the life-giver, but there are no horizontal relationships. In other words, the social structure of this type of congregation is weak. Warp yes, woof no.

That is the situation from which an African church community, the small Christian community, wants to escape. The members experience their old family and clan communities (which are far more extended than the prevailing Western nuclear families) as too restricted and too restrictive.

UNIVERSALITY: GOD'S FAMILY

Everyone who is confronted with the life of Jesus Christ knows that in him a new type of human life appeared. This new type of human life was not accepted by the representatives of the older type of life, and definitely not by those who had organized that older type of life and profited from it. Jesus was seen, and rightly so, as a threat to the status quo. Jesus himself said that it would be difficult for anyone accustomed to the old wine to appreciate the new.

One of the characteristics of Jesus' lifestyle was its universality. He called God *our* Father (and, as our life comes from God, also our Mother). In justifying his behavior before his covillagers and the members of his family in Nazareth he spoke in inclusive terms. He mentioned not only those near him, but also the Sidonian woman at Zarephath, and Naaman, the army commander of a traditional Jewish enemy (see Lk 4:26–27). The people of Nazareth did not like that, and they tried to march him then and there to his death. In Jerusalem he stopped the temple service (an unheard-of scandal and blasphemy) shouting: "From now on *all* peoples . . ." (see Mk 11:17;Is 56:7). The people in Jerusalem did not like that, and Mark says that they came together in the corners of the temple to plot how to march him to his death (Mk 11:18). Jesus told the Samaritan woman at the well not to bother about the liturgical discrepancies between the Jews, who worshipped God in the temple, and the Samaritans, who worshipped on a mountaintop (see Jn 4:7–26). Jesus disregarded religious, ethnic, and economic differences. His universality thus included women, children, invalids, and outcasts. He paid special attention to the exploited, and he refused under all circumstances to let his authority turn into power or violence, to be used against "outsiders."

It is this universality that attracts Africans. They want to be taken up into that new life, a life (as we will see in a later chapter) that is so necessary for them in today's brutal economic, political, and international situation. The African's willingness and eagerness to be baptized has to do with the new economic order in the world for which all people of good will are waiting.

A REORGANIZED LIFE

African Christian church leaders are aware of this anticipation and demand for a more just order. They cannot escape this community demand: as a manifestation of their demands and needs African Christians often begin to form small Christian communities themselves if the imported church structures do not organize them first. The movement in Africa is to separate from the established churches if they are too impersonal, too abstract, or too individualistic. In 1968 Barrett counted six thousand Independent church communities. John Mbiti, former director of the Ecumenical Study Center of the World Council of Churches in Geneva, expects that the number of these communities will increase to about eight thousand by the year 2000.

Even within the Roman Catholic church the inclination is to form small Christian communities. The Catholic bishops of Africa urge their formation, but their realization is sometimes difficult within existing church structures. For the acceptance of those communities requires the development of a new ecclesiology. Kenyan Bishop Raphael Ndingi made that clear when he told the Irish National Mission Congress (Knock, 1979):

> In the past, it was common to picture the church as a triangle with the pope on the top followed by the bishops, the clergy, the religious, and the laity at the bottom. An arrow pointed downwards implying that everything came from the top down. In Eastern Africa, a new suggested approach to ecclesiology is evolving. It is based on the concept of the church as a *communion of communities*, a two-way sharing between communities, while at the same time preserving everyone's Christ-given role within the church, including the roles of the pope and the bishops.[3]

Those communities are essential in the African religious environment. The danger is always that the existing religiosity will remain unincarnated. In the community this incarnation is almost unavoidable. As long as church leaders only preach, the existing order is not in danger. As long as church members are only interested in being charismatically filled with the Holy Spirit, the rest of the world will remain untouched. Services we may organize in order to alleviate poverty do not do away with unjust structures. Even political action alone often remains on the margins of society and does not touch hearts. It is only Christian life in a Christian community that is a challenge and a threat to the unjust status quo. Such a community offers a visible, live, and concrete alternative. If churches would be that kind of church, if they reorganized human life, they would be as serious a danger to the existing order as Jesus was in the world in which he lived and died.

SUBVERSION

It is not surprising that all over Africa churches and governments often connive to do away with the small Christian communities. In his *Pro Mundi Vita Dossier* (November 1979) Michael Singleton wrote:

> There is hardly any government in Africa, whether it is white or black, socialistic or liberal, military or parliamentary, progressive or reactionary, that has no difficulties with the militant, marginal religious movements and that does not feel obliged to take oppressive measures.

Singleton adds that it is also not surprising that the Reverend Shehata of the All Africa Conference of Churches made the following statement in November 1978 at an African church leaders meeting in Kenya: "There are two dangers that threaten Christendom in Africa: Marxism and the sects." He insisted that church leaders should understand the position of their respective governments when they try to eradicate these movements.

In some cases taking measures against these communities is indeed necessary. For example, the communities might create a potential danger for the rest of a population if their members refused to be inoculated against some disease. Furthermore, notwithstanding their potential universality, which could be realized if the communities became part of a community of communities, they often fall into the trap of becoming exclusive, restricted to one people or one class of people. Fundamentally, however, the aspirations of Christians in these communities are spiritually healthy. The communities derive their power from the fact that their members are initiated into the life of Jesus Christ, that they belong to his family, that they want to live his life. Initiated in and with him they belong to the household of God.

5

When Human Life Is the Main Issue

Sixty-five bishops from East Africa met at Saint Thomas Aquinas Major Seminary at Langata, Nairobi, in December 1973. They had come together to plan for the 1980s, and they had a long agenda. One item on the agenda was "The Family and Marriage." Bishop John Njenga from Eldoret (a region in central Kenya) pleaded in his working paper on this issue that the bishops direct more effort toward studying polygamy in Africa. The custom was a pastoral problem because it conflicted with Christian ideas about marriage. The bishops however limited their discussion almost exclusively to the question of whether or not a polygamist who wanted to be baptized had to first send away all his wives (and their children) except one before he would be allowed to receive the sacrament. Even that discussion irritated the Italian Apostolic Nuncio who attended the meeting.

Cardinal Maurice Otunga, archbishop of Kenya, who had recently baptized his polygamous father on his deathbed, observed that he could hardly be expected to condemn polygamy as totally bad and immoral, for he himself had been born into and reared in a polygamously structured family. Bishop Raphael Ndingi said that he could not believe that Jesus Christ would ask a polygamous husband to send all his wives and children away before he could be baptized. He added: "Why don't we go directly and personally to Pope Paul VI to explain the situation to him. If we do, I am sure he too would have to admit that something should be done." At that point the Nuncio, Monsignor Sartorelli, rose from his seat. He interrupted the meeting and asked the bishops present to change the subject. He told them that the pope would be very upset and sad if he heard that polygamy had been discussed. The bishops did as the Nuncio requested. The incident was not reported in the official published minutes of the meeting (*African Ecclesial Review* 16, 1974). There was only brief mention of it in the local Kenyan daily press.

STATISTICS

In October 1967 Pope Paul VI wrote in his encyclical *Africae Terrarum:*

The system of polygamy, widely spread in pre-Christian and non-Christian communities, is no longer coupled to existing social structures as it has been in the past, and fortunately polygamy is no longer the prevalent life-attitude among the African peoples.

In his book *Polygamy Reconsidered*, Eugene Hillman, a Holy Ghost missionary, expresses his doubts as to the accuracy of that statement.[1] According to reliable data, 742 different ethnic groups were living in sub-Saharan Africa in 1967. In 580 of those groups, polygamy was not only accepted but was considered the most satisfactory form of marriage. That means that 78 percent of those people practiced polygamy. In 34 percent of these groups, over 20 percent of the marriages were polygamous; in 44 percent of these groups, less than 20 percent of the marriages were polygamous; in 22 percent, polygamy was accepted but rarely practiced. In Africa south of the Sahara, 35 percent of all marriages are polygamous with an average of 245 women for 100 polygamously married men. If one counts the polygamous and monogamous marriages together, 150 women are married to 100 men. The average number of women per man is 1.5. That means that, on an average, two men are married to three women. This proportion is in line with the actual proportion of marriageable women and men in Africa.

There are several reasons for polygamy. First, there are simply more women than men in the marriageable age group. (In

Guinea, for instance, there are 125 women for each 100 men.) A second factor is the difference in the age of the women and men at the time that they marry. Men marry later than women. In most traditional societies men may not marry until they have "served" for some years as warriors. The difference in age between men and women eligible for marriage is ten years or more. Considering the short lifespan in traditional societies, that age difference at the time of marriage is important. There are always many more women than men.

TO PARTICIPATE IN LIFE

Polygamy is not alien to the West. The European form is different from the African one. In Europe many *consecutively* marry more than one woman or man. In Africa polygamy means to be married to more than one woman *at the same time*. All those who marry after a divorce are in a sense polygamists because they do not restrict themselves to only one partner.

It would be indelicate to state without any qualification that the increasing number of divorces and the increasing number of marriages after divorces in the West is only due to the insatiable lust of the people concerned. But many who speak of Africa say without hesitation that lust is the main reason for polygamy. Even the most enlightened and liberal scholars speak in those terms. In matters concerning marriage and sex, Western theologians readily evaluate the issue in this way.

Hillman has collected an anthology of such statements. Marc Oraison assures us: "The practice of polygamy in one or another society is always a sign of psychological immaturity" (*Learning to Love*, 1966). Ignace Lepp notes: "Polygamy disappeared (among the civilized Muslims in North Africa and Egypt) at the moment they had reached a level of psychological maturity that made them no longer only look for sensual satisfaction, but also, and in the very first place, for something more spiritual" (*The Psychology of Loving*, 1963). Herman Thielicke, in his *Ethics of Sex* (1964) and Bernard Haring (*Marriage in the Modern World*, 1965) make similar remarks. (Haring changed his opinion after a visit to Africa.) Otto Piper wrote in his book *The Biblical View of Sex and Marriage* (1960): "The fact that some people think that it is possible to love at the same time more than one person does not prove that polygamy is as valuable as monogamy, but only that love can be something very superficial." It is almost unbelievable that that could have been written in a book studying the polygamous relationships in the Bible. Was the love between Jacob and Rachel only possible because it was superficial? Saint Augustine (354–430) had, already in his time, an answer for those who underestimated polygamy when he wrote against Faustus:

> It was no crime to marry more women when it was the custom. It is now a crime because it is no longer the custom. In that time it was the normal thing. The only reason that it is not allowed nowadays is because customs and laws forbid it. At the moment, now that our laws and customs have changed, men can only experience satisfaction with more women if they are over-lusty. It is in that way that the misunderstanding arose to think that nobody ever would be able to be related to more women except in the case of lust and sinful desires. Not capable of understanding what might be going on in the mind of somebody else, they compare themselves with those others, just like the Apostle says (2 Cor. 10:12), and it is in that way that they make their wrong evaluations.[2]

Polygamy in Africa is definitely not primarily a manifestation of lust. Many different factors are involved: the difference between the numbers of men and women, prestige, and social standing. In most cases, however, polygamy is simply a function of respecting the rights of everyone to participate effectively in human life. Polygamy involves an element of sympathy, pity, and even mercy. A bride who remains childless in Ukambani, a region not far from Nairobi and populated by the Kamba, will be allowed to marry another woman. This is no printing error: *she* will marry *her*. The two go through all the formalities of a normal marriage ceremony and they together present their two wombs as one womb to the husband. They both become mother if that womb carries life. The only solution to help a young widow to fulfill her life-giving role when all the men of appropriate age are already married is to marry her to a brother of her deceased husband, who, of course, is probably married already. If a young man dies before becoming a father, but at an age when he could have been one, he will nevertheless be married: after his death he takes part in a marriage ceremony. By means of this "ghost" marriage, a relative of the dead man will assure him of offspring. The bride is married to the "spirit" of the deceased. In all these cases, the issue is really the life-fulfillment of the respective men and women. It is not only a question of the life of those who are going to be born; it is also and even more a question of those who are giving life.

After a talk on love and marriage at a girls' secondary school near Thika, an industrial satellite of Nairobi, questions were asked. A young woman of about sixteen spoke. "Is it true that Jesus said that a man may marry only one woman?" The answer given by the European speaker was another question: "Why do you ask that question?" The girl stood up again. The room became very still. She said: "But what if there are in a community more women than men, what are those women who are left over supposed to do? I can't believe that Jesus could have said that they would have to remain unmarried and without children." All the girls started to applaud, shouting enthusiastically to the speaker: "Point, point!" The young woman had indeed made a point, and a point not only applicable to the African communities in East Africa. Polygamy is also an issue in the Goan community. The Goans came to East Africa at the beginning of the twentieth century. They were descendants of an Indian population converted by Saint Francis Xavier. Catholicism is a centuries-old tradition with them. Many of them now are migrating to Europe or Canada. More young men than young women are leaving. These young men marry overseas. Thus many marriageable Goan women in East Africa cannot find a husband.

To that African student in Thika the idea of not being married and of not having children was appalling. It must be clear to the reader by now that for an African to be childless is practically to be dead. One is not taken up in the lifestream. Life stops in those who are childless. They are not only marginalized: they are dying, and at the moment of death they are cast out of the lifestream. How could Jesus, in whom life is created, who is the son of God, ask such a thing? All the students looked at the speaker. What answer could he give? Did he, coming from the West, even understand the question?

Jesus must have been speaking about polygamy in the case of the childless woman. Matthew 22:23–30 tells the story of a woman whose husband died without leaving her a child. After the death of her husband she was "adopted" by the brother of her husband. She was still childless after the death of her second husband, so she married her first husband's third brother, and so down to the seventh brother. It is impossible, considering the importance of marriage in those days, that all those brothers had remained unmarried. Though Jesus must have known about this, he told the story without making any remark against their polyganous state. Onan, in the Old Testament, did not like this custom and he refused *to give life* to the wife of his dead brother. God punished him with his own death because of that refusal (Gn 38:8–11).

It is not the intention of this study to give a defense of polygamy in Africa. Neither is it the intention to defend polygamy as such. It is not even the intention to suggest that the marriage relationships in Africa are ideal. The point is that when Africans are confronted with the Western monogamous marriage pattern, they do not exactly know how to react. Their situation seems to be so different from the Western situation. It should therefore be evaluated in a different way.

Aside from solving the problem of the higher number of women in relation to the number of men, polygamy also has other functions in African society. One of those functions is to build up an enormously varied network of social relations. That social network is considered in Africa to be enriching; at the same time it assures security in times of famine or other disasters. If the family is spread over the whole of the country, a drought in one area is not to be feared so much. There will always be something to eat somewhere. In the West the individual is glorified. Individualism is not highly esteemed in Africa. The ideal human being is for the Masai the person who lives together with and for the others. Among the Gikuyu, individualists are egoists: *persons who work for themselves alone.*

Another reason for polygamy relates to the high rate of infant mortality. How can you be sure to have a son who will in his turn grow up to become a father if you are married to only one woman? That is a realistic question in Africa, where 30 percent of all children die during their first year, and the mortality rate during the following three years of life is sometimes even higher.

In the area of sociability the monogamous family has its difficulties. The "pagans" often laugh at the Christians because they are so inhospitable. A monogamous family with only one woman cannot be as hospitable as a polygamous family with more hostesses.

FERTILITY

The importation of Western Christian monogamous marriage has caused many problems and difficulties in Africa. One of those problems became obvious during a meeting of all the Episcopal Conferences in Africa (Nairobi 1978). The bishops present discussed African marriage and family issues. They seriously debated whether fertility is so important within an African marriage that without children a marriage should be declared null and void. The only laywoman at the meeting managed to convince the bishops to study the question more carefully before making any decision. Would it not be more human in such a case to allow two partners to take a second woman instead of allowing, or even obliging, the husband to send his wife away? Was that sending away not exactly what Jesus forbade? (Mt 19:9). Another consequence of the introduction of monogamy has been the institutionalization of prostitution. The unmarried woman remain "unbound." According to John Mbiti, some African peoples did not even have a word for prostitution before the coming of Christianity.

HYPOCRISY

The African marriage issue has become very complicated. The persons concerned do not know exactly what to do. It is even difficult to get accurate data. The relatively few authors who have studied the problem are usually from the churches. They differ even over the facts. Eugene Hillman states that African women accept polygamy with little criticism, but the authors of *African*

Christian Marriage disagree.[3] All seem to agree that the question should be studied further.

Is polygamy only a temporary phenomenon? If the number of boys born is equal to the number of girls born, will monogamy become the normal marriage pattern? Most authors seem to think so. Many say that biological facts prove the opinion that the natural marriage relation is monogamous. However, the higher rate of mortality among boys and other factors mentioned above probably mean that these biological facts are not unqualifiably applicable to the situation in Africa. In the midst of the confusion and complication that surround the issue of polygamy, what should be done? Should one, because of custom and law that developed in Western Christian culture—where the discrepancy between the number of boys and girls did not exist—make that law and custom apply to all? Would one then not be preferring a man-made law to God-given life? Do not many theologians (for example, E. Schillebeeckx) say that there is nowhere in the New Testament an explicit command that marriage should be monogamous or an explicit prohibition of polygamy? Should those who were polygamously married before they joined Jesus' family of God be refused the sacraments? Must we rigorously adhere to the Council of Trent's ruling—developed in an exclusively Western Christian context four hundred years ago—that anyone who holds that Christians are permitted to be married to more than one woman at the same time, and that this is not forbidden by divine law, should be excommunicated?

These are difficult questions that touch not only Africa but also other non-Western cultures. Even the West may suddenly have to cope with too many women for the men available. In fact that situation existed in some Western countries after the two World Wars. Many of us remember the despair of so many war widows looking desperately for a husband, especially in Germany. Should we rashly judge cases, as those in Africa, in which priority is not given to a law but to the right everyone has to find fulfillment in life? Did not the prophet Isaiah speak of such a situation, and did he not foretell that seven women will cling to one man telling him: "We will eat our own bread and wear our own clothes, only let us be called by your name; take away our reproach" (Is 4:1)?

Hillman writes in his study:

At the present time simultaneous polygyny may be regarded as a problem peculiar to parts of the non-Western world. It is not fantastic, however, to suppose that in the future this could also become an acute problem among Western peoples. Considering their traditional methods of settling international disputes and the sinister potentials of modern warfare (nuclear, biological, chemical), it is quite conceivable that these genocidal techniques, failing to achieve a "final solution," could produce so drastic an imbalance among the sexes that plural marriage would become a necessary means of survival for this or that particular people in the West. Then, contrary to previous custom and law, an overriding natural and moral inclination might arise in favor of polygamy. In such a situation, we may be sure, theologians and church leaders would quickly enough produce weighty reasons and biblical texts to justify a new conception of marriage among their own people. How weighty must the reasons be? How many biblical texts are needed?[4]

At such a time the real priority in any moral context would be rediscovered: human life. This priority often seems lost in some civilizations that refuse to grow because of priorities misplaced, according to some, from the very beginning.

In Africa the church seems to be willing now to study the marriage issue. This is an admission that the last word has not yet been said. But this "admitting" has already gone on for a long time. In the meantime the persons concerned have to find their own way. Who will help them through these difficulties that are not even of their own making?

The evening before Pope John Paul II flew to Zaire the president of that country hastily married a woman he had been living with for quite some time. In Zaire the pope stressed the law of monogamy. He said monogamy was not something derived from the Western way of life, that it was a Semitic custom. That remark was received with some amazement. The Semitic world was definitely polygamous. The old Semitic world, the world of the Old Testament, is much nearer to the African reality than to the Western one.

6

Beginning Only

In September 1975, about one hundred Christians met with their parish priest, Simeon Sawadgo, in the small village of Baam in Upper Volta. They had come together because they had noticed that practically all their pastoral work consisted in the initiation of new Christians. Almost three-quarters of all the time given to pastoral work by the pastor, the catechists, and community members was spent on catechumens.

The people discussed this in their meeting. After their analysis they decided that to continue in that pattern was in a certain way regressive. The catechumenate is in a sense the rear guard; it is definitely not the vanguard. The baptized Christians should call the tune and set the pace. They should be the example of what it means to be followers of Jesus Christ. Almost all their time was spent on newcomers and hardly any time was spent on the people who were already of Jesus and belonged to his family. Priorities should be reviewed and changed. The pastor, the catechists, the men, the women, and the children present asked themselves the question: What is really the most important thing in the lives of those who want to follow Jesus Christ? After a long discussion they thought they had found the answer in a text of the Acts of the Apostles (2:42–47) describing the life of the first Christian communities. They hoped to be able to build a Christian family community along that line.

IN THE BEGINNING

The last time I attended a Christmas celebration in Europe was years ago. It was in a large parish church in Holland. During midnight Mass, the church was overflowing. On a usual Sunday the church was never more than about half full. For Christmas everyone had come. The building was so full that the people in the front had to stand among the life-sized statues of the crèche. The straw in the stable was trampled under foot. Someone had carefully removed the statue of the child Jesus in his cradle to a corner of the stable to protect it from the shifting crowd.

In the sacristy after Mass we wished each other a happy Christmas. The parish priest, visibly glowing with pleasure, said: "It is good to see that they did not lose their good old faith! They all came, didn't they?" The sacristan, an old man who had been working in that church for over forty years, answered: "Yes, but that is the only time of the year that they come. They never have any difficulty celebrating the beginning!"

Missionaries too are very attentive to the beginning of Christian life. In certain regions of Africa nobody is baptized without a preparation of at least three years. In Upper Volta this preparation was the issue of primary importance.

In the West things are different, if only because of the practice of baptizing children almost immediately after their birth. Even in the West, however, the introduction of newcomers is given more importance than the follow-up among adults. A great deal of time is spent on catechism classes, religious instructions in schools, and preparations for first communion, first confession, and confirmation. It is as if one got stuck on the beginnings. Is this perhaps the reason that the most jubilantly and enthusiastically celebrated feast in the Western churches is Christmas: the beginning? Is it not for many the only feast they can celebrate with a good conscience?

In his book *God in Africa*, Malcolm McVeigh, a Methodist missionary who worked for more than twelve years in different regions of Africa, noted that missionaries preached how Jesus Christ had become our fellow human being, but that they hardly ever gave further guidance on what this meant in everyday life.[1] McVeigh refers to a study, "The Growth of the Church in Buganda," by the former general secretary of the Anglican Missionary Society, John V. Taylor. Taylor remarks: "The missionaries are not concerned with that question at all. They are anxious that the Ganda should acknowledge their sin, and the sufficiency of Jesus to cover it." McVeigh adds: "It is always dangerous to generalize regarding missionaries. Nevertheless, it is not a misrepresentation to say that Taylor's observations regarding the situation in Buganda have a validity which goes beyond that country.''[2] This is a remark painful to hear, but one that is often made. It seems as if the more Christian an African country becomes, the more undesirable and "un-Christian" its situation becomes.

But we have to be careful. Europeans say often of difficulties in Africa: How is it possible? How was General Amin possible in Uganda? Africans could with good reason ask the same types of questions about European countries where over 80 percent of the population is baptized. How was Hitler possible in Germany, Stalin in Russia? Let us not forget that many African soldiers served in the front lines in Europe, Asia, and their own Africa during the two world wars. They saw how Christian nations tried to murder and eradicate each other.

THE MISUNDERSTANDING

The missionaries who came to Africa were not isolated individuals. They came from their Western, Christian communities. They had grown up in them; they were rooted in them. They only preached—especially at the beginning of their missionary work— what they had experienced and learned at home. Their message was practically exclusively about humanity's salvation and happiness in another world, heaven. McVeigh rightly remarks:

> Missionary work reflects by and large the ambivalence of the sacred-secular dichotomy of Western culture. While in *practice* missionaries address themselves to the needs of this world—through education, agriculture, medical and social service—their message is principally directed in an otherwordly direction.[3]

The goal of the missionaries' work even had something to do with their interpretation of the miracles of Jesus. Did he heal the blind to give them their sight back for the here and now of this world? Or did he heal them to give us a sign that he had come to make us happy in an eternal heaven to come? Did the missionaries build their hospitals to heal the sick, or did they consider those healings only as means toward another end?

The irony is that missionaries and Africans misunderstood each other completely on these points. In the first place, most Africans had no difficulty at all with the belief in a life after this life. That is something they accepted as a given. In the second place, they were not at all afraid of hell or eternal damnation for the wrongs done during this life. Evil was punished here, during this life. In general (there are some exceptions, especially in West Africa) Africans were of the opinion that the world to come would be a continuation of this world.

When the Africans heard that Jesus had come to deliver them from evil, they did not think first of another world. Most probably they did not think of that at all. Their life-vision focused on this world. They hoped and expected that they would be healed and delivered from the evil spirits that made some of them into alcoholics, spendthrifts, and lechers here and now. If they were childless, they hoped to get children. Sick people had themselves baptized in the hope of being healed.

If there was ever in this world a religious attitude that lent itself to having Jesus and his Spirit incarnated in everyday life, it was this African worldview. It was a vision that needed completion considering the biblical revelation about the nature of the life to come. That completion was given to the African. It was, however, often given in such a way that it neutralized the working of Jesus and his Spirit in this world. One missionary formulated this beautifully, succinctly, and disastrously. Efraim Anderson wrote in his book *Church at the Grass Roots*: "Having arrived at greater maturity, the Congolese plainly understand that salvation means above all entry into heaven."[4] Spiritual maturity accordingly consists in being interested in one's spiritual salvation in heaven. Missionaries unfortunately too often gave that impression. It is still a Christian interpretation that is often preached in Africa, especially by Baptist missionaries from the United States. Kenya has more evangelists of that type now than at any time before. Those evangelists are not without financial means; one asks why and by whom so much money is spent on the spreading of this type of "good" news.

UNINCARNATED

If the only important issue in life is to be saved after this life, the salvation of this world is without significance. The social, economic, and political life of this world can go on, unredeemed, unchanged, unliberated, and unpunished.

Yet Jesus maintained that our political life should be impregnated with the Holy Spirit. He said that those who use power only for their own profit are pagan. Jesus added that politicians should imitate his nature and style and be servants of others and their interests. The consequence of a bourgeois Christianity that is merely interested in the assurance of a chair in heaven and not in the redemption of this world will be Christians coming to church to be baptized in the beginning of life and to be buried at the end of life. In that type of "spirituality," Christmas and All Souls Day will be the most popular and probably the only feasts that are celebrated (as is true in so many Western Christian countries). In the West this reductive interpretation of Jesus and his mission obviously has been possible. Whether it will be possible in Africa in the long run is, thanks be to God, a question.

I wish to end this chapter with a quotation from McVeigh's book *God in Africa*:

> The insight of Africa that life is a totality, that there can be no ultimate separation between the sacred and secular, and that religion must be brought to bear on all man's problems is Africa's great contribution to the West, a belief and faith the West desperately needs. When this is coupled with the Christian recognition that "religion" relates to the Creator God who is near in Jesus or it is nothing, there is achieved the fulfillment not only of religion but life itself.[5]

7

Past and Future Now

A few weeks after a failed military coup, the Association of Member Episcopal Conferences in Eastern Africa (AMECEA) held a plenary session in Nairobi. The meeting should have taken place in Lusaka, the capital of Zambia. The church authorities in Rome, however, had removed the archbishop from Lusaka and had called him to Rome. The bishops were afraid that there might be demonstrations in favor of the archbishop during their meeting at Lusaka, and that is why they decided to meet in Nairobi. A Kenyan bishop gave the sermon during the opening session in the cathedral of Nairobi. He spoke about the relationship between church and state, and between church and justice. It was a good and brave sermon. One of his themes was that the church, though interested in the salvation of this world, never should forget that its first and proper aim is eternal salvation, or heaven.

The following day the sermon was covered extensively in the local press. A taxi driver in an old Ford stopped me in the street. In his hand he had the daily paper with the report on that sermon. He told me that he was not pleased with the sermon. "I thought," he said, "that the church would give us hope," and he added a remark that resembled something the pantheist Christopher Milne once wrote. "Christianity is in the last instance destructive because it stresses heaven so much that this world becomes a kind of camping place, something very provisional."

FORGOTTEN MORALITY

In her doctoral thesis, Hannah Kinoti explored the reasons for the death of the traditional morality of the Gikuyu (one of the

51

larger groups of people in Kenya, numbering three million). That was not her only point of inquiry. She also questioned why that old morality had not been succeeded by a new normative system of ethics. Most of the Gikuyu had been Christianized, yet everywhere were complaints about the morality of the youth and the adults.

The reasons the older generation gave for these problems were especially revealing. They said that nobody took the moral norms seriously anymore because the missionaries and evangelizers always preached reward and punishment in the hereafter. The consequences of bad behavior were thus delayed until after death. All right, that death would come for sure, but why take it into account while you are alive? Formerly, they added, we did not think like this. The punishment for wrong doing followed immediately, in the here and now of this life. One astute respondent traced the difference even to the way Sunday school teachers tell stories with a moral. They tell those stories in a way different from the way we used to, she said. "They will say if you do this or that, *later on* that or this will follow. But we used to say that if you do this or that, that or this would follow *immediately*, while you are doing it. In our tradition, blessing and curse worked here and now; nowadays it is different. You can do what you want without consequences. No wonder people have changed!"

THE STOLEN CONSCIENCE

At the Second Afro-Asian Philosophy Conference, held under UNESCO auspices (Nairobi, 1981), the West African philosopher Wiredu remarked on the ever-growing corruption in Africa.[1] He too blamed the Christian churches in part, but he approached the issue in a different way. He said: "In our traditional African setup we did not know the phenomenon of *preaching*." One did not talk of or preach on morality from pulpits. It was within the context of the concrete, daily life that moral behavior was immediately and directly evaluated. It was a question of consensus.

The danger of disunity in a family at a funeral was, for example, simply neutralized because everything the dead person had left behind was consumed or destroyed by those who participated in the funeral. This also prevented an unhealthy accumulation of goods by some. If a man became so rich that he could build a larger house than the others, he could be sure that his house would be burnt down. When a young woman proved not to be a virgin on the night of her marriage, all the young women and girls of the village would sing of her that she was like "an open cow." Of course these examples cannot be generalized for the whole of Africa, but they illustrate what Wiredu was trying to say.

According to Wiredu, Christianity stole the conscience away from the people. Christianity made that conscience something strange, something alien, something coming from elsewhere. More and more often people say: "How could you do a thing like that; I thought you were a Christian?" Wiredu points out that this shows that morality no longer comes from within the people but from without. Ecclesiastical leaders and most African political leaders (who also preach) speak of justice, integrity, honesty, dedication, commitment, and similar ideals but do not pay the slightest attention to them in their own daily lives. For them, those are ideals that should be realized in a vague, far-off future. Morality is not rooted anymore in humanity. Morality is abstract.

One might of course object that those Christians never understood the indwelling of the Holy Spirit. If that is so, should not the preachers be blamed? Did they not stress the wrong side of the message?

SALVED CONSCIENCES

The popular, conservative preacher will often say that contemporary human beings are losing their sense of sin, and much of the popular, conservative literature of today carries the same message. Those preachers and authors bemoan the disappearance of private confession, and contrast the liberal ways in which the modern faithful measure the gravity of their sins with the ways of an older generation. Is it accurate to say that modern human beings have lost their sense of sin? Would it not be accurate to say instead that their sense of sin itself has changed? Martin Heidegger's thought is similar. He wrote that for persons who really care about *being*, confession of personal and individual mistakes and wrongdoings is not a significant enough experience, because they realize that the guilt for the injust situation in this world lies *at the very root of their existence*.[2]

In an African context this sounds over-individualistic. Yet our guilt does surpass whatever sin we might have committed. It lies much deeper. Did not the spiritual authors of our pious treatises on sin and the composers of our examinations of conscience contribute to a salving and a lulling of our consciences by never helping us to enter into the deeper responsibility we all carry for the hellish situation of our world?[3] Do we touch our sinfulness when we restrict ourselves to confessing an act of injustice or fornication?

When a thief was caught in a traditional Gikuyu community, he was brought before the elders. They did not, however, merely judge and punish the man—they investigated further. They tried to find out why this person felt obliged to steal. According to Gikuyu principles, a just man is one who is self-reliant in caring for his family and who does not bother others unduly. But this presupposes the organization of the community to be such that everybody is able to act in accordance with those principles. Did this man steal because he was simply unjust, and a lazy thief? Or did this man steal because the community he belonged to treated him unjustly? Was his community organized in a way that it did not do justice to him? If this latter was the case, then it was up to society to pay a "fine" to the man in question.

Our peccadilloes are an aspect of our guilt. However, on a deeper level aren't we responsible for the disastrous situation in the world around us, and isn't our guilt for that so profound we cannot even confess it? If God offers us salvation in Jesus Christ, should not that salvation be worked out in the actual world situation? A God who would enter our situation without pointing to the hellish character of it and doing something about it would only be our enemy, our opponent. In the Bible the name for that opponent is Satan. If we insist that the consequences of our behavior and of our attitudes will be mainly or exclusively felt in the hereafter, we not only uproot the foundations of the moral order here and now, we also postpone the coming of the kingdom of God. That kind of belief in the future is merely a poor excuse to do nothing now.

LIFE WITHOUT FUTURE

About ten years ago the Kenyan theologian John Mbiti remarked that his people, the Akamba, had a two-dimensional view of time: a very long past and an extremely dynamic present. "The future as we know it in the linear concept of time is virtually non-existent," he wrote. He thought this true not only among the Akamba, but also with most other African peoples. Numerous African anthropologists, theologians, philosophers, and sociologists were offended by this. They felt that Mbiti's experiences among the Akamba could not be extended and generalized for the whole of Africa; furthermore they thought it likely that Mbiti's statements were not true even when applied to the Akamba.

Mbiti concluded from his studies that the Akamba would never be able to grasp eschatology. He remarked that the manner in which the Akamba interpreted eschatological realities was earthly and materialistic. However, Mbiti did not ask whether the idea of time among the Akamba was different from the New Testament idea of time. Does not John call the time in which we now live "the last hour" (1 Jn 2:18)? In Nazareth, after having announced the kingdom of God, did not Jesus add that the kingdom is *now* (Lk 4:21)? Should not his followers have that same idea of time: "A very long past and an extremely dynamic present"? In the *now* in which the year of grace begins, the kingdom is realized, justice is done, peace is made, swords are hammered into plowshares, and spears are transformed into sickles. If that does not happen *now*, we are unfaithful to him or we are deceiving ourselves when we say that we are his followers. If we only believe, if we only hope that all this is something of the future, we will never realize it at all. It is not so much a question of not being able to believe in the *now* of the kingdom. The issue is our unwillingness to believe. We don't want to believe because we know that everything, our whole lives, would have to change. We don't want that change, and that is why we continue to believe in a future, a hereafter, notwithstanding the fact that that future is nothing else but *now*, the time of this generation. *That time is now.*

And we pray and we pray, asking for the coming of the kingdom, postponing it to a future day, overlooking all Christ's stories that should shape our lives, overlooking God's word *now*: the treasure found, the fish caught, the seed sowed, the yeast kneaded in the dough, the pearl bought, the salt put in, the light put on, the banquet ready, the unwise maids late. The time is now, this is the last hour, there is nothing to wait for anymore. It was all given long ago: aren't we that treasure, aren't we the fish, aren't we the seed, aren't we the yeast, aren't we the pearl, aren't we the salt, aren't we the light, aren't we the guest, aren't we the seven maids on time?

All those who maintain that the year of grace did not come, that justice cannot be done, that peace cannot be made, and that the swords—both the nuclear and the older ones—cannot be hammered into plowshares, into sickles, into food, into education and health—they are not of Jesus' mind. They are not of his spirit, his vision; they are not *his*, whether they are popes, presidents, bishops, priests, or you and me. The lack of interest in a far off future among African Christians, based on their traditional vision, might be a healthy contribution to Christianity.

8

Terrorized by the Written Word

The European missionaries were easily identifiable because of their dress and their behavior. Once they had been the bosses. That is to say, they had come to Africa under the leadership of their own superiors and bishops; no Africans had asked them to come; no Africans exercised any control over them. They had been very efficient and very effective. Their work obviously had been blessed.

Their situation had changed drastically. They were now working under the guidance of African bishops and together with African priests. One reason they had come together was to discuss their relationship to those bishops. They had asked the bishops to give them contracts. Several bishops had expressed hesitation; some of them had simply refused. Nevertheless, the proposed contracts were reasonable. The European priests wanted some certainty and some security as to their upkeep, their medical insurance, their transport, their paid holidays. The bishops seemed afraid of those contracts. Consequently some missionaries were afraid of the bishops.

Somewhere there was a misunderstanding. Bishops and missionaries saw the issue differently. The bishops thought the best "contract" with those missionaries was their personal relationships with them. They wanted to ask the missionaries whether brothers and sisters, parents and children, sign contracts to be sure of their mutual support. Is not that help given, is not that support assured because of the personal relationships between the family members? The missionaries in their turn were afraid of being left empty-handed when some severe situation arose. They had, in a way, the same fear that the bishops had. Those bishops were afraid that the missionaries would leave them behind empty-handed at the end of the agreements, or worse, that the missionaries might cause difficulties before the contracts would expire.

There was another reason for the bishops feeling suspicious. The contracts were not to be between person and person, between a missionary and a bishop, but between the bishop and an institution. It would be possible for the institution to fulfill the letter of the contract by filling vacancies with any available person. The contracts might be kept, while the persons involved could be exchanged and interchanged like things. The bishops wanted personal relationships with the missionaries themselves. They felt that only that type of relationship is trustworthy.

That same feeling is the reason that traditional African parents do not trust the signatures their children put on their marriage contracts in churches or registries if the traditional marriage arrangements have not taken place. Those traditional preparations, the dowry included, have no other aim but to build and strengthen the relationships between the two families and the two partners. Then everyone was sure that the new home was going to be built on the only rock that guarantees faithfulness: close human relationships. These relationships are more important than any other factor in African society. They mean more than written words. They are more important than a contract.

FEAR OF THE WRITTEN WORD

It is remarkable that so many of those who have influenced our world in a lasting way never wrote a word. Socrates did not leave a single written word behind. Buddha did not write. Jesus wrote once, as far as we know, with his finger in the sand. Saint Philip Neri, the founder of the Congregation of the Oratory, consistently refused to answer in writing the questions he was asked. He said that the written word risks becoming a kind of lie. The receiver often takes the written word literally, even years after it is put to paper. He felt the written word to be too fixed, to permanent. As Pontius Pilate once said: "What I have written, I have written.'' He said this when some priests and scribes appealed to him. Their appeal fell dead against the solid written word.

The Evangelists were inspired to write many different stories about Jesus, and that prevented a fundamentalist fixation of that living person into one set scheme. Because the four canonically recognized reports vary, Jesus lives in our considerations. Our Christian ancestors, who decided to authorize four stories, must have known something of the human distrust of the written word.

Ancient Greek authors, Herodotus for example, claimed that the Ethiopians had invented the written word. Later research has uncovered many examples of ancient, written African languages. Yet the written word rarely was used in sub-Saharan Africa. African students often express surprise at the paucity of the written word in their cultures. They ask: Why did our forefathers and foremothers never write?

Many answers have been given to that question in the course of the years. Some have suggested that there were too few inter-cultural contracts to serve as catalysts in the development of the written word. The information necessary for survival could be managed within an oral tradition. Others are of the opinion that trade had not developed to the point that the people needed the help of a complicated administration—replete with invoices, statements, and written accounts—as seems to have happened in the Middle East.

THE LINEAR WRITTEN WORD

It may be that those cultures that did not develop the written word did not need it for their communication system or did not want to rely on it because they experienced life in a way different from cultures that did develop literacy. The work of Marshall McLuhan has influenced many scholars to view literacy and illiteracy as key factors in determining the course of a culture's development. One of McLuhan's theories holds that the written word breaks up human communities. Before reading and writing developed, McLuhan hypothesized, all information was passed on orally (or in Africa over the longer distances via drums). Information belonged to everyone. It was public. Everyone had (in principle) access to the same data. When persons in a community started to read and to write, a series of new developments took place. These developments were strengthened by the invention of the printing press. As a result of these developments an individual could build up a personal information bank, independently of the rest of the community or of any other individual. The whole of reality, up to then seen as one coherent world, was *seen* as being broken up into different words. Up to then a person "named" reality with different words, it is true, but after the development of the written and printed word one could *see* on the page how reality consisted of "things" and "persons" separated from each other. The old unity broke up and was replaced with alienation. Members of the community became strangers to each other. Even their relationship with the surrounding world changed. Under the influence of the written word, and especially under the influence of the printed word, the whole life-concept changed. Each book has a beginning and an end, and a logical, explanatory development between those two. Life was thus falsified. Utopia was born. Logic ruled over intuition, and in the linear written and printed word, the playfulness and the tortuousness of life was falsely straightened out.

CLASS LANGUAGE

The written word made possible the development of languages independent from the life of the community. The language of the specialist, the language of the theologian and the creed, the language of the law and the contract, and the language of those who were formally educated all developed. Theologians created religious jargon and used it to contradict each other; bishops used it to censure theologians. The faithful were left helpless in the religious cold of everyday life, even though theological discussions were only possible because the faithful paid for the upkeep of the bishops and theologians.

Almost all information was held in common in the old African community. There were, of course, exceptions—in the arts and some crafts, for example. The African community did not need to preserve its knowledge in libraries and reading rooms. Everyone knew everything. The fact that the language was not written hindered (at least theoretically) the development of a highly stratified class structure. The technical, noncommunicative scientific languages, the written, printed, or photocopied memoranda in the closed archives of the West have restricted information and knowledge to the class of the knowers, the specialists.

René Bureau, in his book *The White Danger*, writes:

> In that time reading and writing was invented, a tool in the subjection of humanity. Decrees and orders got an irrevocable character, and became law in immeasurable spaces. The living, spoken word was directed towards feedback, it remained always within interhuman reach, it was nuanced; now the word was stultified, petrified, killed. At the same time reading and writing narrowed the entry to knowledge much more than it widened it. It created an upperclass that started to refuse to do any manual work. The "elite" had been born.[1]

A new struggle began.

The struggle is apparent in Africa even in simple situations. One example: An American priest-counselor was introduced in a student parish. He had had the best possible training in his field. He said that he had to be paid for his services. Some thought this an unusual demand for a priest to make; he felt it was necessary in order to attain the correct client-counselor relationship. He reduced the fee to a minimum: a dollar an hour. Finally some people with problems were willing to pay. The form required before the counseling could start was filled in with much hesitation. At the moment that the counselor started to take notes, even during the counseling session, all trust and confidence fell away. That should not be done. How could he do that? How was he going to use those notes? Would others have access to them? Was he writing a study on his clients? The specialist gave up within a few months. He could not find anyone interested in his counseling. He never understood why. The fear of the written word made his work impossible.

At the beginning of this chapter we noted the preference of certain African bishops for human relations rather than contracts. The same fear and preference can be found in African theology. The theories of McLuhan, though developed in a different context, can help us understand. McLuhan suggests that the spoken language is "hotter" than the written language. He means that more senses are involved in the case of the one who listens than in the case of the one who reads. The listener sees, hears, feels, and can even smell the speaker. The reader only uses sight to look at the print on paper.

Feelings and even thoughts can be better expressed by the spoken work than by the written or printed one. It is not without reason that we read poetry aloud to ourselves, even if we are alone. Speakers also see us, the listeners, and they can notice if we understand or not, if we are getting upset or falling asleep. This feedback is important to the speaker. In reference to this and other related issues, Desmond Tutu, the Anglican archbishop of Johannesburg in Azania, writes:

> Too many of us have been brainwashed effectively to think that the Westerner's value system and categories are of universal validity. We are too concerned to maintain standards which Cambridge or Harvard or Montpellier have set even when these are utterly inappropriate for our situations. We are still too docile and look to the metropolis for approval to do our theology, for instance, in a way that will meet with the approval of the West. We are still too concerned to play the game according to the white man's rules, when he often is the referee as well. Why should we feel embarrassed if our theology is not systematic? Why should we feel that something is amiss if our theology is too dramatic for verbalization but can be expressed only adequately in the joyous song and movement of Africa's dance in the liturgy?[2]

We might ask ourselves whether this is true only of Africa. More and more of the faithful in our Western countries are avoiding the endless words churned out in liturgy and theology. But nobody in the West has invited the faithful to a dance—there does not seem much left to dance about.

9

Different and Yet the Same

As Pope John Paul II left the cathedral of Nairobi after having been received enthusiastically by the priests, sisters, novices, postulants, and seminarians, it started to rain. It was a real cloudburst accompanied by lightning and thunderclaps. The cheering crowd scattered into doorways and under protruding parts of the buildings, but they continued to cheer. The rain was seen as the sign of God's blessing upon the arrival of the pope in the country.

In Europe or America rain is not a sign of blessing. But in Africa, where every harvest and consequently human life depends on rain water, rain is seen as a blessing. This rain was a special blessing because a drought of some months threatened the crops of the country. Long lines before shops selling staple foods were a daily sight in Nairobi. That rain contributed more to the success of the visit of the pope than anything else. When a Dutch reporter explained at the immigration office of the airport that night that he had come because of the visit of the pope, the immigration officer said: "You are very welcome, the pope brought us rain."

That rain created some confusion, however. The gifts that had been given to the pope as he left the cathedral almost fell into the water. Some Sisters of Charity had come from far away and intended to sleep in a convent in town. They had brought their own food with them, nicely packed in paper. While the heavens lit up with lightning and the rain renewed its attack, the pope hurried along, accepting presents from right and left. He saw the sisters, greeted them quickly, and with a beautiful smile took their lunch parcels, thinking they were gifts intended for him. The sisters did not dare to protest. Nobody knows what the reaction was when those gifts were unpacked in Rome. Nor does anyone know what happened to the two goats that were offered, according to local custom, to the pope during the offertory of the Mass. The last thing heard was that they kept the pope awake that night, because, bound to a tree in the garden of the nuncio, they did not stop bleating through the whole night.

PARADOXES

The visit of the pope was a success. Millions came from all over Africa to see him and, if possible, to touch him. Many in the churches of Nairobi and Kenya had been praying that the visit would be a blessing for the country and for the pope. The visit was a success, notwithstanding the fact that hosts and guests did not always understand each other.

Both parties must have been struck by the sometimes paradoxical situations. For example, on the eve of the pope's arrival in Zaire, President Mobutu called the whole diplomatic corps of Kinshasa to the cathedral to witness his Christian marriage. When the diplomats entered the church, they were confronted with what seemed to be two brides. Both were dressed in the same way, both had the coiffure traditionally worn at the marriage ceremony. Mobutu married one of them. The other one was a sister of the bride, but according to local rumor those two sisters had given Mobutu four children over the last two years. What happened really in that cathedral that night?

A member of a European television team commented: "The more he [the pope] travels, the more confused it all becomes." An anthropologist of the University of Nairobi said, during a reception a few days after the pope's arrival, that the pope unavoidably was going to suffer the paradox that hits all professional anthropologists at one time or another: the paradox of observing that every human group is identical to the group to which the anthropologist belongs and that at the same time everything is different.

CENSORSHIP

The instances of paradox were legion from the beginning of the trip to the end. Upon his arrival at the Nairobi airport, the pope spoke to the youth. There were thousands of them. Practically every school child in the capital had received a card on which was printed: "The government of Kenya invites you to come and greet the pope at his arrival and at his departure." The pope told the young people that he knew how numerous they were, that he was aware of their dreams, and that they could count on his understanding, in everything. During that short speech he was interrupted by applause and cheering thirty-five times.

When, next morning, a representative of the Kenyan youth, a student from the university and the national chairperson of the Young Christian Students (YCS) addressed the pope, he did not keep to his original text. In that text, written by students, he was to have said: "Please, Holiness, look once around yourself. Do you see all the faces of those white priests? They are very welcome, and they do a good work. Yet, we would like to have our own priests, and some of us would like to become priests. But we Africans like human life so much that celibacy is a real obstacle. Would you be able to take that into consideration?" He did not say that at all in his speech. Someone had censured his talk. Another end to a dream of the youth.

In his speech to the youth, the pope said: "Be yourself and remain yourself," a theme he often repeated during his trip through Africa and later during his talks to African bishops at their quinquennial visit to Rome. But he did not commemorate the last supper of Jesus Christ in a real Zairean liturgical context. He told the Zairean bishops that he understood their desire to be totally Christian and totally African but that the two could only be harmonized under the supreme direction of the Holy See and the universal church.

How can what really differs be concurrently the same in all its forms of expression? In Kenya the question remained. In what capacity had the pope come to visit? Did he come, invited by the president, for a state visit? Or did he come, invited by the local hierarchy, for a pastoral visit? Nobody knows, and nobody will ever know. In his farewell speech, the president of Kenya, Daniel arap Moi, asked the pope to greet the people of Vatican City in the name of the people of Kenya.

Maybe because of this mystery, the pope muddled the continuing local discussion on the role of the church in politics. He spoke about it in his sermon during the open-air Mass in Uhuru Park.

About a million people were present. First he said that Jesus' mission was neither social, nor political, nor economic. He added that the mission Jesus gave the church was neither social, nor political, nor economic. Then he said that it would be wrong to think that the individual Christian should not be busy in those important fields of human life. At the end of his homily he said that the political life is a great challenge for each Christian. The confusion was such that the coordination committee had to ask for some clarifications in the text before they dared to print it in their official commemorative album.

HOPE

Little enthusiasm was shown by the people during that sermon in Uhuru Park. It was a poor sermon, not adapted to the crowd. The pope did not tell a single story; he did not repeat ideas or statements; and he read the whole speech. He was interrupted by applause only once—when he spoke about corruption and extortion. The same thing had happened in Zaire (where President Mobutu had left the ceremony at that point). It was significant that this was the only time the people applauded. The applause indicated what those hundreds of thousands expect of the pope and the Christian community: an alternative world without corruption and extortion.

African corruption goes very deep, but certainly not as deep as in the West. In Africa it affects the ordinary person in the street, who may be stopped by a police officer for one or another flimsy reason and required to pay a bribe of a dollar or so. The story goes that one cannot get access to one's bank account in Nigeria without a tip to the clerk behind the counter. It is said also that in Zaire people who do not put some money in their postal box every month will receive no mail. In Kenya it is practically impossible to get a driver's license without paying some *chai*, some "tea," a bribe.

That type of corruption cuts to the very bone of the ordinary person. It is also the cause of an enormous anger that could explode suddenly in Africa. Everyone knows of their leaders' bank accounts in Switzerland. The Church starts where men and women are filled with God's promise of justice for all and are looking for supporters in view of this messianic message. So when the pope broached this topic, the people applauded and whistled loudly, and looked over their shoulders to see whether "the big fish" were listening. The pope was seen as a sign of hope at that moment, as the fighter for an honest and just alternative. Here too, however, the whole situation was paradoxical. The pope was invited by the national leaders he accused. When Mobutu left during the ceremony, he showed who was the stronger.

WHAT IS THE USE?

There were many other paradoxical situations. It was in Nairobi, the heart of Africa, that Pope John Paul met a group of Hindus for the first time. It was in West Africa that he first met with the archbishop of Canterbury. There were too many other similar situations to mention here. There were bitter accusations about the proselytizing character of the pope's trip. The Muslim leaders in West Africa did not come to listen to his speech there.

The pope went home (in as far as those Vatican buildings of suprahuman proportions can be called a *home*) dead tired. That is what he said, as he stood the day after his return behind his high window overlooking Saint Peter's Square. Maybe he asked himself the question journalists from all over the world had asked local priests in Africa: Would it not have been better for him to have stayed at home?

In Africa this question does not make much sense. The fact that the pope decided to come to visit was seen by the hundreds of thousands of people who came to see him as an honor to them. It is quite something in Africa when an important person visits your family. His visit was clearly seen as a sign of hope—hope in a sometimes hopeless situation. The hungry too had come to see him. Perhaps that was why about a thousand people fainted during the open-air Mass in Nairobi.

Here again is a paradox. After his arrival the pope was greeted by a disabled child; immediately after that, he was busy for about an hour with the representatives of the diplomatic corps and the prominent people of the country. Some in the crowd whispered: "He is just like all the others!" His visit could have been organized in such a way as to stress hope. In Kenya he did not see a single slum area. He spent his nights in one of the most elegant parts of town. He did not go upcountry. He did not see Kenya's misery, but neither did he see Kenya's riches—its people.

He must have noticed the paradoxes. He even helped people to think about their culture. He must have learned a lot. What conclusions did he draw? During his visit the American weekly *Time* reported that it foresaw great changes in the African church. Would Christian developments in Africa remain faithful to the directions from Rome? Will Rome take those developments into consideration? Up to now no sign of such consideration is apparent. On the contrary, it seems that there is a concerted effort to establish the ways of the Western church in Africa and to nip in the bud any revival of a contemporary African culture.

One thing is certain: the solemn and serious character of the papal Mass was thoroughly interrupted in Africa—in Zaire by colorfully dressed dancing seminarians, in Kenya by two goats. It is difficult to do something about life; it is so alive. It breaks rules all the time. And things that are the same really differ.

10

Community Power and Institutional Impotence

In 1976 the representatives of the episcopal conferences of Tanzania, Uganda, Kenya, Ethiopia, Malawi, Zambia, and Sudan met in Nairobi. During their meeting the bishops declared that the only way to humanize and Christianize the world is to form small Christian communities. In 1977 they received support for their opinion from the Synod of Bishops in Rome. The synod stated: "The ideal way to renew parishes is by changing them into a community of communities."

It was no news to East Africa that the imported, territorial parish system could not be the definitive pastoral structure in Africa. That structure proved to be impossible territorially because each main parish had dozens and dozens of outposts. Socially it proved to be undesirable because the enormous parishes with the consequent weak interpersonal relationships between members did not correspond in any way to the great desire for communities in which one would be really bound together with others. That type of community had always formed in Africa when survival was threatened. It was the type of community needed to counteract the breakdown of the old family and clan structures—a breakdown caused by all kinds of alien influences, missionary Christianity included. The thousands of Independent Christian church communities that have split off from the traditional, "colder" mission churches are living proof of this tendency.

NO LUXURY

One of the research projects in the Department of Philosophy and Religious Studies at the University of Nairobi consisted in interviewing those men and women who were considered by their people to be "wise." In Kenya about thirty such persons had been identified. It was not difficult to find them. Everyone knows the local philosophers.

Among them was one Luo elder named Oruka. He was asked, among other questions, for his ideas on traditional community structures. He said that they were disappearing. When asked why he thought they were disappearing he gave an unexpected, pragmatic answer. He said: "Our community spirit disappeared because we no longer need it. Formerly, in the olden days we had to do things together in order to survive. We needed each other to defend ourselves against wild animals and human enemies. We had to share our food together to remain healthy. We had to organize ourselves and to divide our workload in order to live. All those things are not necessary anymore. Everything has changed. Everything is organized in another way, and the whole of our community has collapsed."

He looked somber and sad as he said this. That sadness must have caused him to forget what he had said some minutes before, when he gave a different reason for the existence of the old community. He had explained that in the traditional setup the whole of human life was interconnected. Life came through ancestors, forefathers, and foremothers; life came through your parents from God, and it was handed on by the living to their children and their children's children. It all hung together. It was all interrelated. The members of the old community were kept together in two interlocking ways. They belonged together for two reasons. There was that common, inclusive life that came *from within* the community; and there was that need to keep together in view of the dangers of the world *from without*. The old community was no luxury; it was a life-condition.

PRIMITIVE CHRISTIAN COMMUNITIES

When the Spirit of Jesus descended visibly for the first time in human history over a group of people in Jerusalem, those people immediately formed a community. They had to; they had no choice. They had all received the same Spirit and the same life *from within*, and they suddenly had become strangers in their own world, which now threatened them *from without*. They lived as the Jews once lived in Egypt. In that context the Acts of the Apostles uses the word "parish" (*paroikia*: dwell as strangers) for the first primitive Christian communities.

According to the reports on that first community, which was brought together at Pentecost, the members of it did everything together. They prayed together; they ate together; they solved their "apartheid" problems together. They shared their goods, and they offered in that new community a lifestyle that in its organization and spirit was totally different from the pagan world.

In the Greek town of Ephesus this alternative grew so strong that it became a threat to the local economy and even endangered the tourist industry. The mighty Roman Empire saw those Christian communities as a threat until the new situation of the post-Constantine period. Once the heart of resistance, they then became the bulwark of the status quo.

ACTUAL SITUATION

The East African press reports almost every day on religious communities that come into conflict with the modern world around them. Members of these communities refuse to be inoculated. They refuse to send their children to school. They do not bring a dying man to the hospital. They do not want to be counted during the census. They refuse to take off their turbans when they are to be photographed for their identity cards.

These people justify all those refusals by appealing to special group revelations, to their being healed and counted by God, to the circumstance that they are no longer living on earth but are already in heaven. Or, appealing to an instrument of the modern world, they cite the constitution, which guarantees freedom of conscience. They are often arrested, fined, and, as they refuse to pay their fines either on principle or simply because they do not have the money, imprisoned.

That kind of resistance is negative. There is, however, an element of sincere concern about a situation in which forces and powers of the modern world attempt to manipulate the members of these groups. They refuse to be manipulated, and they feel (and know) that their resistance can only be organized in a community.

In August 1978 missiologists from all over the world came together for a conference at Maryknoll, New York. In the papers presented at that conference one hardly finds evidence of the old motives for mission. The command to "go, teach and baptize" no longer refers only to the baptism of individuals. It refers to all aspects of human life. One thing remains as before: We continue to live in a pagan world, a world in which human beings are not yet for each other the main ingredients, a world without love for God and without love for our fellow beings. Human beings have not reached yet the point where we understand that our love for ourselves and for each other is more important than any sacrifice or any other interest. Ulrich Duchrow explains this insight in a paper called "The Spiritual Dimension of the Scientific World." I mention only two points from this paper.

Duchrow's first point is that we live in at least two "times." First, there is our biographical time—the time in which we live; the time in which we are born, grow and die; the time in which there is, according to the Bible, a time to weep, to laugh, to embrace, to withhold, to be silent, and to throw stones. That time is subjective and personal. It even has its own personal biological rhythms. Second and next to that time, or all through it, there is a time in which we are forced to live because of modern progress, techniques, and the appointments on our calendars—an impersonal, objective, and objectifying time, a time that again and again breaks through our biographical time, frustrating, maiming, and killing it.

The second point in Duchrow's paper is that we as individuals are all the time manipulated, counted, checked, brainwashed, controlled, and influenced by all kinds of forces in the modern world. The spokespersons for these forces say they wish us only the best; and they do, but not because they love us (or God) but only because they are thinking of their own profit.

We live indeed in a pagan world, and the missiological question par excellence is how are we going to be liberated from it. That liberation will have something to do both with changing the structures in which we live and with changing the manner in which we live our own lives.

In the West we seem to be accustomed to all the interference in our lives. When we build, we are obliged to go to an architect and to the town authorities. When we are sick, we go to a doctor and a hospital. When we want to pray, we go to a church building. We rely all the time on the techniques of others.

In Africa all this is new. In Africa one experiences the opposition between the two times in which we live much more acutely. The tension is to many intolerable and the manipulation (even in ecclesiastical circles) unendurable. The amount of drugs Western society uses indicates that the "habituation" of the people has been paid for dearly.

LIBERATION

Those missiologists who met in New York thought they had found a solution to all those difficulties. The solution was to organize local communities. Their description of the role of those communities corresponds almost exactly to that noted by the African bishops when they came together a year later in Zomba, Malawi (1978).

Within those communities interpersonal relationships are related to the whole of human life, to human life in its totality. Every person (*persona* meant originally a role in a theatrical play) plays his or her role. The old African community did not know of unemployed or marginal people. Everyone had a task, however humble. The African bishops spoke of the presence of the Holy Spirit as the go-between in a small Christian community. It is within such a community that God is Emmanuel, God with us. Within those communities individuals try to analyze their situations together with all those who suffer under similar conditions.

In this way everyone cultivates a political and social awareness, through which each one will be better able to read the signs of the times and respond to them.

This approach is not an intellectual exercise; it penetrates the water and the blood, the marrow and the bone of society. It is not a flight, an escape from reality. Our church communities have been organizing for escape for centuries and centuries. Within and through those communities we want to reorganize and reorient the world so that it may become a real civilization of love.

The small African communities are trying to do this, sometimes in clumsy ways, but they are trying. Often they do not have sufficient insight to understand where the manipulating, frustrating, and negative powers are hiding. They need to get into contact with the Western basic communities that are facing similar structural and personal problems. Whether these contacts can function within the official church structures remains to be seen.

The American Jesuit Daniel Berrigan remarked that the original community-oriented and apostolic spirit of almost all women's congregations in the United States has been eroded by "the blight of the buck."[1] Church structures are often exactly the types of structures that the small Christian communities would like to bring down in our world.

THE POPE CAN'T DO IT

Every time the pope visits a country, his plane is met by the most sophisticated, ferociously murderous fighter planes of the air force of his host country. That seems strange; in a way it is even a scandal. Does the pope not always come as a messenger of peace? But he cannot prevent this display of force. That is why the institutional church, which the pope represents and guides, needs other communities—smaller ones, freer ones—that can do something at their level to promote peace and justice. Even the least materially gifted and privileged small Christian community is spiritually and morally more important than all the official ecclesiastical gestures. It is in those communities that the world is changing by becoming ever more human and divine.

11

The Year of the Jubilee

The Gabbra are a nomadic people in the Northeast of Kenya.
They live in one of the driest areas of East Africa. In 1981 they
celebrated their year of the jubilee, ending another cycle of fifty
years in their existence. In the year of the jubilee crooked affairs
are straightened out, injustice is righted, debts are settled, cattle
(the only property) are reallotted and sins are forgiven. This is not
a myth; it is not a story; it is not an ideal that they believe should
be fulfilled. It really happened in 1981 after a year of preparations. Considering the rapid encroachment of Western life-
patterns, the Gabbra year of the jubilee may have occurred for the
last time, but in 1981 the Gabbra managed to keep to their old
tradition.

The year of jubilee, the fiftieth year, is also part of biblical
tradition. When Jesus presented himself for the first time to his
covillagers in Nazareth after his baptism by John, he told them
that the definitive holy year had started. But, as Israel seems to
have done all through the centuries and especially since its return
from the Babylonian exile, so the people of Nazareth resisted the
idea of the holy year. They did not want it. They even tried to
march Jesus to his death that very same day. There was a reason
for that resistance, especially among those who were in one way
or another in power. When in the beginning of the holy year the
ram's horn (*jobel*) had sounded, the land had to be expropriated
("God alone is the owner of the land"), bonded servants had to
be freed, debts had to be remitted, and justice had to be restored

all through the land. Those in control never wanted anything like that.

AN ADAPTED PEOPLE

The Gabbra are a people that live a most precarious existence—not only because of the grimness of their natural environment, but also because of the disasters and sicknesses that have terrorized them over the last century. Harold Miller, a Mennonite missionary who studied the history of the Gabbra, surveyed those calamities in his article "Jubilee 1981 among the Gabbra."[1] All kinds of sicknesses, once unknown to the Gabbra, afflicted both humans and animals. In 1876 the Gabbra were struck by cholera, in 1879 by polio, in 1890 by rinderpest, in 1891 by smallpox, in 1904 by measles and whooping cough, and in 1914 by six diseases that decimated their cattle herds. In 1880 and 1900 they fought bloody wars with invading neighbors. Finally they suffered a terrible drought in 1915.

Notwithstanding these enormous hardships, the Gabbra survived. The life that continued was selective. The survival of the fittest had been the rule. That is why the Gabbra are physically so well adapted to the life they live. Tall, slim, and muscular, they can walk miles, if necessary, to another pasture should drought come. They are not only physically adapted. They are also adjusted philosophically, scientifically, religiously—in one word, cosmologically.

The number seven is a key number to the Gabbra. They use a cycle of seven days in a week, and fifty-two of these cycles constitute a year—just as in the West. They also think in cycles of seven-times-seven years. The first year of a cycle has the same name as the first day of the week. The first year of such a cycle would be called (in English) Monday, the second year, Tuesday, and so on. Those cycles are, however, not thought of as a linear spiral coming from the past and going into the future. For the Gabbra the seven years and the seven-times-seven years run in a circle. Thus they do not "lose" their years; the years are kept together in their cycle. Every fiftieth year is a special year, an extra one. The year after the seven-times-seven they proclaim a year of jubilee, a year resembling the jubilee year of Leviticus 25. Cattle are exchanged;

differences that have grown out of proportion and threaten to break up society are levelled; quarrels are settled.

WHY SEVEN-TIMES-SEVEN

Miller gives several possible explanations for this seven-times-seven period. Some anthropologists say that for a community without a written language it is easier to keep track of cycles of seven years than it is to keep track of cycles of ten or one hundred years—the system used in the West. Others suggest that it has to do with the biological rhythm in human life. The years *seven* (when, according to church law, one comes to the age of reason), *fourteen* (in many cultures the age to marry), *twenty-one* (the year once used to mark many forms of legal adulthood in the United States) have clearly not only a biological but also a sociological significance. In primary cultures one might add the year twenty-eight. Twenty-eight was in East Africa the average age of the population, and one was supposed to be a grandparent by then. Some nomadic people circumcise every seven, or every fifteen, years. Every seventh year a new generation would be initiated into adult life.

Others suggest climatic reasons for the pattern of sevens. Weather patterns are easy to observe over periods of seven years; lean and fat years are said to succeed each other in periods of seven years. Joseph's dream at the court of Pharaoh must have come to him from a kind of collective memory of this probability. Within such a common memory stories, fables, dreams, myths, and beliefs are born. Everyone thus has something to depend upon, even in the most difficult periods. Those myths insure survival.

The Gabbra use other rythmic time-patterns along with the seven-year cycles. In this way they keep control over an environment that is, in fact, unpredictable.

JUSTICE

Even if we knew the exact origin of the seven-year cycle, another question would remain unanswered. Where did the Gabbra get the idea of the fiftieth year? Was it something that traveled southward from the Middle East of Old Testament times? Was it a custom that the people left in the Middle East when they migrated southward? Nobody knows, but specialists are beginning to suspect that the origins of the Old Testament can be traced to peoples, now living in sub-Saharan Africa, who once migrated from the north, from Arabia and surrounding regions, to the south. This migration continues even in our day.

How did the idea come about to connect the fiftieth year to a restoration of justice and peace? Is that connection also due to the kind of collective memory we mentioned above? Do we know by nature that injustice and violence grow over a period of seven-times-seven years to such an extent that we have to change something in order to continue?

This insight is not lost completely in the West. There too the fifty year cycle is celebrated in golden jubilees. The jubilee is celebrated in many Christian regions in a religious context. A parish priest in Europe told me: "They do not come to church anymore. But at the beginning of life and at the end of life, and at all the jubilees in between, they come. Most family and business jubilees are still celebrated in church."

The ideas of reconciliation, peace, and justice are not part of Western celebrations. That is even true of the celebration of the jubilee year in the Roman Catholic church. The medieval popes, who reinstituted the custom of the jubilee year, spiritualized and individualized those celebrations. They renewed the old custom, but they also betrayed it by focusing the celebration upon individual conversion and the possibility of gaining a plenary indulgence.

In 1300, the first of the new jubilee years, the faithful had to visit Saint Peter's Basilica and the Basilica of Saint Paul-Outside-the-Walls thirty times if they were residents of Rome, fifteen times if they were not residents of Rome when they wanted to gain a plenary indulgence. In the same year Pope Boniface VIII published a decree announcing that the jubilee would be celebrated every first year of a new century.

Reports from historians tell of the enormous crowds that visited Rome during that first jubilee year. The success of the year (from the financial as well as the spiritual point of view) was so great that Pope Clement VI later decreed that the jubilee should be celebrated every fifty years. Pope Urban VI reduced the period between jubilees to thirty-three years (the supposed length of the life of Jesus). A third holy year was celebrated in 1390, a fourth in 1400. The church officials had come to like the special year. When the Vatican announced its most recent jubilee year in 1983, it had to defend itself against the accusation that the year was planned because of the Vatican's poor financial condition. Accurate or not, the accusation was based on precedent.

IN FORCE

Is the celebration of jubilee years as practiced in the Catholic church justifiable? Did not Jesus announce in Nazareth that he was starting the definitive year of grace? Another question might be asked about the way in which the year is celebrated. Should we not learn from the Old Testament and from the example of the Gabbra that the celebration of the jubilee year is not only a question of individual conversion and the gaining of spiritual benefits, but that it should also touch the here and the now in which we live?

It is a pity that an age-old custom that is able to move a whole people like the Gabbra—*from within*—loses its power and force when it is decreed from without. When bourgeois theology starts to manipulate a people's religiosity, the end of all official religiosity is near. The religiosity of the people will go underground.

12

Children's Theology

In November 1980 a number of church historians, called together by the World Council of Churches, met in Basel, Switzerland. They came together to celebrate the five hundred fiftieth anniversary of the meeting of the Council of Basel convoked by Martin V. The meeting in 1430 was an important event, but it has been almost completely forgotten because of the way in which historians have treated it.

The church historians of 1980 planned to discuss the teaching of church history. One of the many proposals of this conference was that church history should not be considered as the mere description of what happened to popes, bishops, kings, emperors, and abbots. More attention should be paid to the people of God and their experiences.

The same suggestion could apply to our studies of what is happening in many countries of the world. We read about the leaders who organize imaginative and inspired rescue and rehabilitation efforts. We often overlook the true source and inspiration of those activities.

LEAVING HOME

In Kenya many things have changed since the government has extended free education through seventh grade. In 1975 free education was given to students only up to fourth grade, when they are about ten years old. At this stage, thousands and thousands of children had to leave school. There was no academic future for them. Their parents could not pay the school fees or buy the obligatory school uniforms. The cleverest boys and girls were hardest hit. During their schooling they had picked up some ideas about their future in upcountry life. They saw the poverty at home. There were too many children; the available land had already been subdivided too often; even the parents were desperate and often told their sons to fend for themselves. The children knew that in the rural areas their future was bleak.

On a clear night the young people could see the far-off orange-pink cloud of the lights of town in the distance. They would sit in the dark corners of those nights when people came back from the town and told their stories. Because only those who had been successful in town came back, all the stories the young people heard were stories of success. So hundreds of boys decided to leave home. Sometimes they walked distances of over a hundred miles. Sometimes they walked for over a week, traveling early in the morning and late in the afternoon, avoiding the dark of the night and the heat of the day.

CITY OF DREAMS

When they arrived in town, all their dreams seemed to come true. The boys who had arrived before them showed them the marketplaces, where the large containers distributed by the city council were filled with discarded food. Along the streets they found garbage cans containing small quantities of cold porridge, old chicken bones, and stale bread. Bread!—a luxury they had never enjoyed at home. They learned how to sell two or three salvaged tomatoes for some money. They discovered that car owners easily could be intimidated while they were parking their cars and asked for money. The owners always gave them something for fear that the boys would pierce their tires or scratch the paint of the car.

After only a few weeks of walking and sleeping in the streets, things turned sour. The boys clothing—never washed—practically fell from their bodies. Sleeping together with boys and girls who had been in town for a long time, the newcomers picked up all kinds of diseases, from scabies to syphilis. Life became grim.

They all learned something else: how to escape from all their troubles. If they were quick enough, they could get the last drops of gasoline from the muzzle of a gasoline pump immediately after its use. They caught those drops in some filthy rags. Then they stuffed the rags inside old milk cartons and sniffed the gasoline vapor. It made them high. They saw figures and colors, angels and God. For a time they were in heaven.

Then the police would come. The youngsters would be kicked and beaten, arrested, and brought before court. They would be put on buses and transported back to their home areas; but at the first stop outside the town, the boys would jump from the bus, sell their tickets, and return to town.

LOVE REGAINED

These boys who came to seek their fortunes soon finished up a sorry sight. They got dirtier and dirtier; their health deteriorated daily; their skin was riddled by mites. But their greatest deprivation was their lack of love.

Finally action was taken. The plight of these young people was recognized. It was decided to try to bring them together, but this was a difficult task. They did not trust anyone and when approached would run away like wild animals. They only trusted the gangs they themselves had formed. Few of the children were older than twelve or thirteen. At last they were brought together in an ingenious way. They were willing to come to parties. So parties were held at the university chaplaincy. A band started to play at noon and played on until 3:00 P.M. After the parties the young people were advised to go to the Red Cross for a wash and a medical checkup.

Schooling was what all the youngsters said they wanted most. This was natural, for some of the most intelligent of the youth had run away from home. So a school was started. It was an informal school, a free one. The students could walk in and out whenever they felt like it. The beginning of the school was so informal that it was called by the name of its first full-time teacher, Tina.

Gradually an alternative educational system has been developed in the school in cooperation with the Kenya Institute of Education, but especially in cooperation with the young people themselves. Their feedback proved all-important. The children simply did not come to school when they thought one or another topic irrelevant. Though some of them hoped to participate eventually in the formal school system, they all understood that a realistic type of education that would prepare them for survival in the situation in which they would be obliged to live was more important.

Within the framework of this approach a new type of religious education evolved too, if only because practically all the children, even the most derelict ones, had picked up a Christian name and had some vague allegiance (without any clear relation to a denominational group) to Jesus Christ—this notwithstanding firm roots in their traditional African religion. A minority, mostly those from Muslim backgrounds, had never heard about Jesus. It was hoped from the beginning that the alternative approach might help the children in the religious orientation of their difficult lives.

THREE LEVELS OF EXPERIENCE

The boys and girls made it very plain that their experiences in life had to be taken into account. This meant that the normal religious education programs, designed for school-going, settled (bourgeois) children, would be of no use to them. They wanted something adapted to them. Three levels of experience had to be taken into account: the existential experience of the children in their precarious environment; the traditional experience of the children—they had been brought up in largely traditional environments; the visionary, prophetic, and transcendental experience of being assisted by people who believed in Jesus—this combined with the students' knowledge, however rudimentary, of the Old Testament and of the life of Christ. The new approach was organized into a three-year program.

METHOD

The course leads the child to the knowledge that humankind—like the child—is in trouble; that solutions can be found to problematic situations; that in Jesus Christ problems are tackled and overcome; that after Jesus' death and redeeming resurrection people created communities to realize his type of life. The syllabus repeats this "lesson" for life each year of the three-year cycle.

Storytelling is the method used. Isn't it through stories that human values and attitudes are transmitted? Isn't it only in the concrete context of human life that one can prepare for that life? The traditional African educational system depended almost entirely on stories, after direct human experiences such as initiation rites and other ceremonies. The teachers in the school are therefore advised not to resort to imported gimmicks such as films, flannel boards, and tape recordings.

In the first year the student is told stories of how God gave life to the world and gave his life to humankind; how this human life went awry when humankind disobeyed God; how after the fall Adam gave Eve her name and started to "rule" her; how Cain killed Abel; how the acquired technology was abused (the tower of Babel); how human relationships were nearly totally ruined (Noah and the flood). These stories are accompanied by the corresponding African stories. The pupil sees how the events told in the stories are still developing in the world of today: the disobedience, the exploitation of women (the prostitution, for example, which they all know), the murders, the arms race, the breakup of families.

Into this context Jesus is introduced—the one born as a new human beginning and announced by John the Baptist, the one who from the beginning was a refugee, a slum-dweller ("what good can come out of Nazareth?"), and also the victor over the temptation to give in to any economic, political, or spiritual power play.

The second year tells of God's new beginning in Abram (who received from God the name Abr-a-ham to indicate that what happened to him should be repeated in everyone). Abraham had to leave his old town, his old ways. He was willing to sacrifice his son; he promised faithfulness to God, who promised to be faithful to him. God gave life to his barren wife Sarah. That life went awry in the case of Jacob and Esau; Joseph was sold by his brothers into Egypt. All the Hebrews ended up in Egypt, and Joseph helped them.

Esau's jealousy of Jacob and the selling of Joseph by his

brothers are real to students, who see nepotism, tribalism, jealousy, and corruption around them. The traditional stories about jealously and hatred are told.

Against this background Jesus' life of healing and reconciliation is told and his visionary description in the Beatitudes of the new world is explained. This Jesus ran the risk of being detained and killed by the established order—a possibility every Third World child knows about.

In the third year the story begins with Moses protesting the exploitation of his people by foreigners and by each other. He tried to lead the people through the desert into a new land, not only spatially but also morally. In the time of Jesus corruption set in once more (the same type of corruption that still ravages our land). Jesus resisted it.

Consequently, Jesus was arrested after his last shared supper. He was killed (all this can be put in a recognizable context in Africa and elsewhere—think of Stephen Biko, Martin Luther King, Tom Mboya). God saved Jesus from death and proved through his resurrection that Jesus' lifestyle is the one willed by him and therefore the true one. The apostles received the Spirit of Jesus, and they formed communities.

The children are told that baptism initiates us into that new life of sharing and that we sharers and companions should realize Jesus' life in our days as an answer to the world's problems. We hope that those who already belong marginally to a Christian community might become a leaven, and that the others who do not belong to such a community might find one.

POSTSCRIPT

Slowly things took shape. Social workers and volunteers found the families of some of the children. In some cases a reconciliation was arranged, but in most cases this was not possible. The children had run away from situations in which they really could not live.

Gradually it evolved that almost no young children were seen in the streets during school hours. This was partly because of the care given to them by Christians but also because of the government's expansion of free education to the seventh grade. The change in the educational system came about largely because of those "parking boys."

The names of the people who organized the children, who took them off the streets, who opened schools for them, who started a reception center and so on, will surely, and rightly, never be forgotten. Some of them for example, Father Noud Grol, a White Father who founded Undugu, have gained international recognition and have been decorated. But we should not forget that it all began because those country children opted for a more just and fulfilling vision of life. Their names will be forgotten, but their crusade was won.

This does not mean that the problems are solved. The youngsters who now come to town are older. They are too old to search the garbage cans for rotting fruit. They have developed their own, less pleasant, techniques for survival. They too need a crusade.

13

The People's Priest

He had been away from home in boarding schools for fifteen years. He had gone to Rome to be ordained by the pope. (Rome likes to prove its ecclesial universality by multicolor ceremonies.) Now he was home again. Although he had been trained for a long time, he was too young to be an elder or a leader in Africa. To the Africans he was like a child—he had not married. And he was going to remain a child; it was said that he had promised never to marry and never to beget children. Yet he was going to be called "father."

It was decided to do an "emergency operation" on him. He was going to be a chief ecclesiastically, so why not make him an elder of his people. This privilege was normally given to deserving people when they became grandfathers. The ceremony took place immediately after the priest's first solemn Mass in his parish. All the parishioners had come for the occasion. He received all the symbols of an elder: the staff, the hat made of the hides of colobus monkeys, and so on. Now he was sitting there in front of them all, with clear eyes, tight in his young skin, shining between the elders. He did not feel at ease; everyone could see that. The elders did not feel at ease either. What had been the intention of this performance? One could sense discord, a misunderstanding. Where?

THE COLLAR AND THE CASSOCK

Much research has been done to explain the decline in vocations to the priesthood. In Western countries literature on the topic is endless. All kinds of religious leaders have had their say. Slowly a pattern has emerged as a result of all the studies and analyses. It is not my intention to enter into the debate. I want only to note the experiences of the faithful and the priests in question.

In the West, priests began to dress the same as other men. They wore ordinary trousers, shirts, and suits. In Africa it was the same. Later, priests worked in factories; some became journalists; others went into politics. Some withdrew completely from the clerical status, saying that they thought they could work better at furthering the kingdom of God in that less obstrusive way. They found the clerical life too distant, too far from normal life. They no longer wanted to be so exceptional.

There were some who did not want to change. In East Africa the Opus Dei priests continued to wear beautiful, heavy, black and white cassocks with enormous sashes. They suffered in the tropical heat, but they did not mind. They thought it worth the trouble. Why did they think it worth the trouble? If you ask them, you will find that their answers correspond to the words used by Pope John Paul II when he obliged the clergy in Rome to wear clerical dress. The hierarchical character of the church should be visible. One Opus Dei student pastor in a campus of an East African university gave a further explanation. He said: "The collar and the cassock work like the conscience of the faithful. When I meet students, my clerical collar and my cassock work on their memories. They will remember where they went wrong over the past days and nights!" The reaction of the students, however, was different. They asked themselves and each other: "Why does that man walk around in those pretentious pieces of clothing?"

NO EXCEPTION

Who would want to be conspicuous nowadays? More and more priests ask themselves in the confessional boxes and before the altars: How can I stand here so apart, so exceptional, so conspicuous, in the name of a God, who became a human being to be inconspicuous in this world?

The example given at the beginning of this chapter shows an attempt to age a young priest artificially, to make him acceptable as an elder. It is possible that the elders, who introduced him to their wisdom and dignity, wanted to show that he was no different from them. From a pastoral point of view this possibility is the most interesting one. It is a possibility that has become a necessity in our church community. Everywhere in the world Christian communities are led by persons who are not priests. Sometimes appearances are safeguarded because female or male religious substitute for the priest. Often that is not possible. Then lay persons substitute. Sometimes those leaders too want to be considered special. In most cases, however, all members participate and rotate leadership. Aren't we all brothers and sisters in Christ? Aren't we all living with the Holy Spirit in us? Church legislation and the learned considerations of historians and sacramental theologians fail us here. They cannot do much about the situation in any case. The faithful will come together to celebrate the event of Jesus Christ whether the official hierarchy likes it or not.

THE LAST ONES

East African daily newspapers now and then print the photographs of traditional priests who have died. The report that this man or that woman was the last priest in a very old line—the last one to know exactly why, where, when, and how certain sacrifices had to be performed. Usually the photograph shows the priest with all the priestly paraphernalia around him or her. In a modern newspaper it looks a bit silly. There is little respect left for these priests, for the "business" for which they were once needed has long been taken over by other management.

It sometimes happens that such photographs appear in the same paper with a photo of a bishop, a cardinal, or the pope. The question comes to one's mind whether those figures will one day disappear like the priests of the traditional African religions. Within the Christian communities of Nairobi such questions are sometimes put sharply—not by everybody, but by some. Catholic students are troubled by other students: "Why are you always going to these priests to ask what you may and may not do? Although many independent church groups take the hierarchical system with them when they leave the established church, more and more of these groups are antihierarchical. But even the antihierarchical groups cannot completely escape the old system. Some time ago a letter was sent around from the Nairobi deans to warn pastors against a new antihierarchical sect. The sect sent some of its members to Catholic churches to receive Holy Communion and to bring the consecrated hosts back for their own celebrations.

The small Christian communities contribute to and influence these developments. Sometimes the impression is given that these communities exist everywhere and that they are one complete success story. That is not true. Bishops often pay only lipservice to them. Even that helps. Responsibilities that up to recently were entrusted only to priests are now delegated to the small communities. Consequently, existing communities are beginning to act more independently. They organize the liturgy; they prepare the sermons; they compose hymns (different ones for each Sunday); they read and apply the Bible texts, and at least on paper they are responsible for the choice of their pastors. The bishops of East Africa stated at their general meeting of 1979: "Candidates for the priestly and religious life should be recommended by their local communities."

Another growing influence is that of the pentecostal or charismatic groups. To be touched by the Holy Spirit within those groups is an experience that is nonhierarchical. It can happen to men or women, to elders or children, to lay people or priests (in fact it does not happen so often to priests at all).

One of the documents of the Second Vatican Council, the *Decree on Priestly Formation (Optatam Totius),* speaks of two priestly models. Some tension exists between the model of the priest standing apart as a spiritual power source with exclusive and exceptional prerogative and privileges, and the model of the priest who remains a member of the community. It is not difficult to see which model will prevail in Africa in the future. Who then would want to be a priest according to the old model any longer?

HARDLY ANYONE

The answer to that question is very simple: hardly anyone. The fact that the seminaries in East Africa (there are not that many) are full does not mean that all those students want to become priests. The seminary is for many students the only way to continue their studies. The students who want to become priests are usually the ones who have no objection to a type of training that still works according to the old model of the priest. They are the ones who accept the hierarchical structure within the seminary. Student unionism in seminaries is looked upon with great suspicion, and many students who have lobbied for some say in the matter of their training have been sent away.

Priests who have been educated according to the power-source model get into difficulties when they are appointed to communities that are more at home with a people's priest, a community priest. The local press reports regularly about foreign and local priests who refuse people baptism and communion, who do not allow certain coffins to be carried into their churches, and who excommunicate parishioners. In many areas of East Africa more than 80 percent of the faithful are not allowed to receive the sacraments because their marriages have not been validated in the church. They feel that marriage is their affair. The number of Christians who marry in church is, except in some towns, smaller every year.

The expectations of the small Christian communities seem to conflict with the type of priest the seminaries produce. The crisis is so serious that the Eastern African Episcopal Conference asked the pastoral institute at Eldoret in Kenya to investigate the matter. Their study is on the role of the priest in the Christian community in Africa.[1]

Some attempts have been made, mostly in Tanzania, to change priestly training. The stronger the small Christian communities in a diocese, the more that need for change is felt. There has not as yet been a real breakthrough. Rome stands officially by the old model, and Rome is still paying most of the costs of the seminaries. The piper plays the tune of the one who pays him. The Institute for Higher Ecclesiastical Studies that Rome started recently in Nairobi is a copy of a Roman pontifical university.

A CHANGING CHURCH

A changing church of course also alters its priestly model. As it is not yet clear what the changing church will become, it is not clear either what the priest will become. One thing, however, seems sure: it is useless to perpetuate the old model—not because spirituality, faith, or commitment are lacking. It is simply that no one can work anymore with a priestly model that functioned well and responded to a felt need in the past but is now unacceptable. That is good; it means progress—a feudal ideal is disappearing. The lack of vocations for that type of priesthood is a blessing.

Young people who feel a vocation to the old priestly model are not only a difficulty; they are a disaster. Bishop Antonio Celso Queiroz, auxiliary bishop of São Paolo put it another way:

> Historically, the priest was practically the factotum (do-all) of the church. . . .He must rediscover his role as a community coordinator. . . .Not that the priest is to be blamed for a historical situation. But it would be blameworthy if now he did not have the sensitivity to perceive the signs of the times and the Spirit speaking to the church. So it is not merely a question of the priest stopping one activity to perform another, or changing a style of dress! He has to review the way he exercises his mission within a new theology of the church in which the key words are community and coresponsibility.[2]

No wonder that the face of the young priest who was sitting between his elders looked like a big question mark. There he was, separated from his agemates, quickly and artificially "aged" by people who wanted to show him that he was not above them. Would it not be better to reserve the priesthood for men and women who have proved that they can exercise the type of leadership that does not put them above others? Would it not be better to encourage toward the priesthood those who have demonstrated that they can exercise an authority that functions *within* the community and not from *above* it or *outside* it?

Officially the bishops of East Africa agree. One of their theologians, Father Brian Hearne, wrote:

> The bishops of AMECEA have laid down guidelines for the church in their policy statements of 1976 and 1979, and opted for a Church where the gift of God's communion is made manifest in communion among people, rather than for a Church based on impersonal institutions and organization. They have seen small communities as the best means

of renewing the Church, of bringing people to a living faith, of getting them involved in the life and the mission of the Church, and of making the Church into a transforming force for the whole of society.[3]

This new model of the church calls for a transformation of ministerial structures and attitudes. It calls for a transformation of the seminary system, not only in East Africa, but in the whole world.

14

Spiritual Imperialism

He had been attached to a well-known pastoral institute in Central Africa for fifteen years or so. The institute was known not only for its residential courses, but also for its extension work all over Central and East Africa. It had published several studies on religious, theological, and liturgical renewal in the region. Many of those studies had been written by Africans, but the great majority had been done by expatriates. The teaching staff of the institute had been almost completely Western all through the years of its existence. The official explanation for this was that the bishops of the region did not have sufficient local personnel to be able to assign any of them to nondiocesan work.

He was a participant in a discussion. The topic of discussion was interesting. Recently several different congregations and religious institutions had come to establish themselves in the region. Someone in the group spoke of these groups as "the spiritual multinationals." The Jesuits had come and within three years owned beautiful residences in town, two of them used as retreat houses. The Benedictines started by building a huge convent and a church so big that the local cathedral was almost dwarfed by it; the church was so richly decorated that some people living in the neighborhood never went to it—they thought their clothes were not good enough for their huge parish church.

Capuchins from Malta, Franciscans from all over the world, White Fathers, Holy Cross Fathers, Camellian Fathers, Salesian Fathers, Dominican Fathers, Verona Fathers—all had come, not just to cooperate in the existing missionary and pastoral work, but also to do what they called "discreet animation and promotion." That is to say, they were all out to fill their (often depleted) ranks with young recruits and novices from Africa. Some of them immediately opened novitiates and juniorates in Africa or in Europe for those aspirants. Even the older congregations, who had been working in the regions for years and years, became involved in recruitment. In some of those congregations and societies the average age of their European and American members was over fifty. This did not keep them from participating in the struggle for life and for survival.

Not only the old established orders were represented. The latest religious and spiritual foundations in the church came to Africa. The Opus Dei from Spain and South America founded some exclusive colleges. And more came: the Focolarini from Italy, the Neo-Catechumenate Group from Spain, the Marriage Encounter from Ireland and the United States, the (somewhat older) Legion of Mary, the Taizé community from France. . . .

The discussion centered on the effect on Africa of introducing all those different spiritualities and movements from Europe and America. Was it not at the cost of local initiatives? Does any of those Western spiritual schools take account of African spiritual traditions and inspirations? The word *transnationals* was used over and over. Then the director of that pastoral center spoke up. He said, "I do not really understand the difficulty; in my view there is no African spirituality." It became suddenly very silent. The director had vast experience and should have known what he was talking about. He did not doubt that one could discuss whether or not there should be *one* spirituality for the whole of Africa. That might have been a good question. He doubted that one could speak of any African spirituality at all!

DENIAL

The General Secretary of the World Council of Churches, Philip Potter, who is West Indian-African, stated in an interview in a Dutch weekly *De Tijd* (September 1980):

Racism is the tendency to reject others because they are not as we are. I saw that early on in my life; that is why I decided to dedicate my whole life to the struggle against all those factors that hinder us from accepting the differences in each other. Everything I have done in my life is centered on that issue.[1]

One of the ways by which this racism, as Potter calls it, betrays itself is by trying to make others exactly as we are.

When members of the new societies and congregations started to infiltrate East Africa, it probably never entered their minds and hearts that their lifestyle and spirituality might be different from the cultural and religious values already present there, that an idea like "holiness" might mean different things in a Western and in an African context. Having always lived in their own environment, knowing hardly anything about human possibilities in other cultures, they thought their own ways universal. They considered human life in all its cultures to be one and the same. What was good in Rome or in Madrid should be good enough for any other place in the world.

If you asked those groups about this attitude, probably the missionaries among them would be the first ones to suspect, at least in theory, that there might be differences. In the practice of the missionaries' apostolic activity and life, however, the differences are often overlooked, organized away. It is true that the older missionaries especially had a great interest in the cultures they met. They did much valuable research. The intention of that research was too often to know African customs and values better in order to counteract them more vigorously.

It has proved difficult even in the West to continue the traditional ways of Christian life. Yet, without any ostensible hesitation, these same ways are pushed on the minds and hearts of the people of other, very different cultures. One example is the priest-model of the Latin Church after the Council of Trent. There of course must have been a reason for the existence of this model in that Latin Church. For theological and spiritual reasons, it is a model in which an African young man (the woman is excluded) can hardly be happy. The Africans' worldview and appreciation of life conflict with the model.

Even in the West that old priest-model is on the way out. The old ideal with its feudal oath of faithfulness to authority, its obligatory celibacy, its endless periods of initiation in novitiates and scholasticates, and its special dress and privileges that stress class consciousness does not have much chance of survival in the very church where it originated. This type of priest-model dates from another time, another society, and another culture—a culture that appears strange not only to an African, but also within its own Western environment.

MONOPOLIES

Again and again it is proved that the Western world dumps its obsolete goods on Third World markets. Drugs that may no longer be sold in the West continue to be produced for the so-called developing countries. We must be cautious with the comparison, but is not the West doing the same in the spiritual field? Many complain in the West that the older spiritual organizational patterns do not seem to work anymore. They do not seem to have much attraction for modern youth. Is it then fair to try to propagate them elsewhere? Is it wise to entrust future religious developments and inspirations to those antiquated forms of spirituality and its structures?

Some of the societies and congregations mentioned above were born in the modern Western world (the Taizé Community and the Opus Dei, to mention only two). From the perspective of other continents, they grew from strange Western soil. Is it any wonder that a rumor is spreading that there is a well-thought-out official church policy to work as fast as possible on the total Westernization of the ecclesiastical world before it is too late, before the non-Western cultures would be able to organize a concerted resistance against those impositions? Does Jesus Christ not offer himself to all cultures, to all families of men and women? Was not the first discussion between Peter and Paul, the man who would later reside in Rome and the man who called himself the apostle of the "pagans," exactly on this point?

If it is true that the older missionary congregations do not attract youth anymore, the church has to look for new forms in order to be able to remain faithful to Christ's mission to "go out and teach!" It would be not only unwise but even ethically wrong to continue to entrust that mission exclusively to communities that are relics of the past. The church has to find new forms; it has to adapt.

It is questionable whether such adaptation will be possible. Is it possible to graft eighteenth-century spirituality on today's life-experience? If that is a question in the Western context, it is even more a question in the context of other cultures. In 1980 Eugene Hillman published *The Roman Catholic Apostolate to Nomadic Peoples in Kenya.*[2] His aim was to investigate whether the methods in missions founded after the Second Vatican Council were different from the methods used before. Except in sporadic cases, he found there was no difference. Hillman describes how children from nomadic peoples were marched to church, even before they were christened, to pray the rosary every day, sometimes in front of the exposed Blessed Sacrament. Before they entered the church, they had to dress themselves in white robes—they were not allowed to enter the church in their customary attire. Adults were only allowed in the church dressed in Western clothes. Nowhere was any local food used for the celebration of the Eucharist. The offerings that were eaten and drunk during Mass were so alien to these people that they did not even recognize them as food and drink. In many cases the missionaries were convinced that a nomadic people could not become Christian until it had given up its nomadic existence and settled in one place.

During the course of the discussion described at the beginning of this chapter, someone asked whether it would be good and beneficial to recruit African members. One response was: "Those African members might be able to bring about the necessary changes." This is like suggesting that merely increasing the number of African priests will result in change in the African church. As things are structured now, this hope seems no more than wishful thinking. All aspirants have to undergo a cultural conversion before they are accepted.

We face here the same dilemma Pope John Paul II faces when he visits Africa. He says that the African church must maintain its African charisma, that in Africa Jesus Christ is an African; at the same time he prescribes his own Western ideas on the church, discipline, liturgy, and even family life.

TO LET GO AND TO KEEP

Before we can appreciate the possibilities in other cultures, we have to understand our own cultures. In his book *The Crack in the Cosmic Egg*, Joseph Pearce describes how our thoughts and our feelings structure the reality around us.[3] Pearce describes how we human beings are capable of constructing or projecting alternative structures or alternative worlds. As he puts it, we live in different cosmic eggs. He argues that it would be ridiculous to assume that people from within traditional Indian or Chinese cultures would view flying to the moon as a desirable event or would imagine themselves undertaking such a voyage. In the West, however, people view flights to the moon merely as a logical consequence of the culture.

The denial of the existence of other cultural possibilities also keeps us from changing our own culture. Before we can accept another culture, we first have to break through our own cosmic egg. That is difficult because it is in that egg that we live. It is still difficult even after we begin to doubt that our egg is as perfect as we once thought it to be. That doubt will help us to break through the shell that surrounds us. That shell does not seem to offer us protection anymore; it threatens to suffocate us.

We have no right to use our rich and powerful multinationals to impose our way of doing things upon other cultures. One of the difficulties in Africa is that too often we have been dominating the local cultures. Without any respect for the older existing situation, we have tried to impose something new. The result is religious and moral confusion.

In his book Pearce refers to a story sometimes attributed to Saint Luke. On the Sabbath Jesus was walking with his disciples in a field where a farmer was binding together sheaves of grain. Jesus already had been in trouble over the law of the Sabbath with the protectors of the existing order. He knew that a civilization and culture depend on the observance of their prescripts and regulations. That is why he halted in front of the working farmer and told him: "If you know what you are doing, be blessed. If you don't know what you are doing, be cursed."

Do the spiritual invaders know what they are doing when they seem neither to respect nor to understand the distinctive features of African culture? They are asking others to let go of everything, but they themselves are not willing to let go of anything. This attitude can only lead to chaos.

Jesus said: "Whatever you loose on earth shall be loosed in heaven" (Mt 16:19). Was that not at the same time a promise and a threat?

15

Forgiveness in Community

A confirmation ceremony was to be held in a Christian community a few kilometers out of town. The bishop had not been able to find his way. The Christians waited for him. When he finally arrived, the chairman of the community asked him whether he would be willing to give general absolution. The answer was No. The chairman then asked whether the bishop would be willing to hear private confessions. Because of the large number of people, the late hour, and other circumstances, the answer was again No. The answer was understandable, and yet we might ask at such a time where ecclesiastical dignitaries get the courage to reduce Christ's words "If you forgive any man's sins, they stand forgiven" to nothing.

MATHEMATICS

Church authorities who would restrict the forgiveness of sins to private confessions heard by ordained priests should start to count. We all learned mathematics in our schools, how to add, subtract, divide, and multiply. We don't apply these simple calculations sufficiently in ordinary life. Just imagine that the church leadership could convince the faithful that serious sins can only be forgiven in private confession (this in fact is the law), and that, convinced of this, the faithful would line up in front of the confessional boxes to wait for their turn. How would we manage, considering the number of Catholics and the number of priests available? There would not be any official ecclesial forgiveness for most of the people. There would be no time to make decisions to forgive or not to forgive; there would be no time for those judgments at all. Within the Christian community reconciliation would officially fall flat. That is what has happened.

CONSEQUENCES

The impractical management (or nonmanagement) of reconciliation in a community cannot but have the most serious effects. Reconciliation is not only a matter between the sinner and God. Reconciliation has to do with our fellow human beings and even with the environment. Reconciliation is about all those relationships. Forgiveness is the only means we human beings have to make the past good again. We have no other way, no other possibility. This leads to another difficulty.

If the power of forgiveness and reconciliation are restricted to one group, forgiveness and reconciliation are going to be neglected. When this occurs in a community, everyone— Christian and all others—become alienated from what they have done and from what they can and will do.

COMMUNITY

All this is the more noticeable in a region where ecclesiastical influences are only about fifty years old. Vincent J. Donovan, a Holy Ghost missionary in Tanzania, wrote a book about his contact with the Masai.[1] He studied the issue of forgiveness among that warrior tribe. For the Masai, reconciliation has to do with their fellow human beings.

If a son offends his father, that sin disturbs not only the relationship between the two, but also between the young man and the rest of the community. The "sinner" is banished from the community. He lives as an outcast a marginalized existence outside the *kraal*; he is not even allowed to participate in the military training of his peers. He brings a curse on everyone with whom he comes in contact. Misery to him, misery to all the others. No wonder that the agemates of the father ask the old man for the spittle of forgiveness. Spittle is something holy, as it is a direct indication of life, especially in a semiarid area. Spittle is not only an indication of life; it is also a sign of blessing and forgiveness.

The father one night climbs a hill or a mountain to ask God in prayer for the spittle of forgiveness. Sometimes the prayer is heard; sometimes it is not. If the prayer is heard, that news goes immediately to the son, whose agemates then in their turn try to convince the boy to ask his father for forgiveness. If the son is ready to do so, his agemates accompany him back to the *kraal*, where his father, surrounded by his agemates, is waiting. The two approach each other. The boy asks for forgiveness, and the father spits on him with the spittle he had obtained from God to the great relief and joy of the whole community.

It can also happen that two families offend each other. This is disaster, a direct threat to the survival of the whole group. If the community falls apart because of a quarrel, everyone will be in danger. No coordinated defense will be possible against enemy tribes or wild animals. Everyone in the community consequently is interested in a reconciliation. All members of the community try to convince the two families to make peace. If they succeed, the two families prepare food. Common food is called *endaa*, but this special food is called *endaa sinyati*, "holy food." Encouraged by the rest of the community, both families bring their food into the middle of the *kraal*. There they exchange their food and eat it to the great jubilation of all. The eating reconciles them. Life can go on.

NO PRIVATE AFFAIR

A private confession to an outsider, however sacredly ordained, would make no sense in such a context. Lambert Bartels elaborated on this theme in his article "Reconciliation and Penance: A View from Ethiopia."[2] In it he presents his study of the Oromo people, who number about a million. With the Oromo, sin is not in the first place something that has to do with God. It has to do with their fellow human beings. Within their frame of reference, Jesus did not come to reconcile us with God, but with each other. God does not punish. Where there is sin, God withdraws from humanity and because of this human relations deteriorate. The *Lineamenta*, an official preparatory document for the synod on penance (1983), stated that "Christian penance is essentially something personal, but it has social implications and consequences" (21). Within the African context such a sentence should be changed to: "Penance and reconciliation are essentially social events, but they imply personal consequences." Both aspects—social and personal—should be respected in that order.

The Oromo celebrate penance by using symbols, which, according to them, are given by God to humanity for that purpose. They sprinkle each other with water; they touch each other with special plants. The community is reconciled, and they are all saved. In ecclesial celebrations of penance, the participants are asked first to reconcile themselves with each other, through one or another gesture, after which the priest forgives them in the name of God. In all these cases forgiveness is granted by the participants themselves, who first pray to God for the power to be able to forgive.

THIRD PARTY

As we saw in the example of the Masai, not only those immediately in need of reconciliation have a role in the process of forgiveness. The whole community is involved. One might say that every reconciliation needs a third party. This is even true in marriage. In traditional African society, husband and wife rarely blame each other person to person, face to face. Ugly family quarrels in front of the children and in front of others are thus avoided, even when grievances are serious. The two speak, each one in turn, through a third party, a person or a group of persons.

In the urban areas of Africa these mediators have disappeared. The result is that necessary reconciliations *cannot* take place. To go and confess to a priest does not help. Some small Christian communities have tried to organize "councils of elders," who listen to the complaints of the two parties and who try to counsel them. After the counseling the official reconciliation often takes place in a church or in the Christian community. If either one or both of the parties confess, it is often done in public. The priest (if present) gives the absolution as a kind of confirmation from God.

Is there a place for such developments? It seems that the church still finds it difficult to realize what *Lumen gentium* stated:

> Particular churches have a legitimate presence in the ecclesial community, enjoying their own traditions, and leaving intact the primacy of the Chair of Peter. In its presidency over the universal assembly of charity, it stands guard over their legitimate differences, and at the same time sees to it that the particularities, far from damaging unity, are a positive service to it [13].

We are far from the realization of that ideal, though the words were formulated more than twenty years ago. If the Roman church cannot appreciate the particularities of Western church communities like the American and the Dutch, how is it going to relate to churches from cultures with which it has so much less in common?

Why all these difficulties and hesitations? Is the answer to be found in the fact that those who come together to discuss these issues (after having appointed each other) are bearers of a power they are not willing to share? Did not Jesus give all power to everyone? But even this underestimates what he wanted to make clear. At the moment that his listeners wanted to stone him because he called himself the son of God and forgave sins, he said: "Is it not written in your law, 'I said: You are gods'?" (Jn 10:34). The story goes that when the first evangelizers entered East Africa (near Mombasa in 1846) and preached that Jesus is the Son of God and that he could forgive sins, the inhabitants there said: "We too!" Did not Jesus come to reveal the extent of that possibility?

16

So Many Myths

Some time ago a new subject was introduced in the curriculum of the Kenyan secondary schools: environmental education. It was to be expected, as the headquarters of the United States environmental program is in Nairobi, Kenya's capital. Environmental experts from all over the world came to Kenya. The syllabus for the new course was developed with the assistance of some of these experts. They opted for a scientific approach. Pollution processes would be explained in different ways and the students would learn what to do about them.

The aim of the syllabus was also to cultivate in the students a sense of responsibility for their natural environment. The effects of water and air pollution would be shown, and the youth would thus be encouraged to take care of their environment. The syllabus included lectures by the teachers and discussions by the participants. During those discussions it became manifest that the African participants possessed a level of experience of their environment that was deeper than the scientific and moralistic level of the material offered. The boys and the girls differed radically on what may be done to the environment and what may not.

THREE MYTHS

The African, Judeo-Christian, and Muslim traditions contain myths about creation, nature, and humanity. In the African stories human beings are the center of all creation. Everything was made for them. But everything was made according to an order, according to laws fixed by God. Interference with that order—by a hunting party, by the cutting of wood in the forest, by the melting of iron from ore—must be done very circumspectly. If something goes wrong with the regular succession of dry and rainy periods, Africans feel themselves responsible. They feel they can't disturb and disrupt nature without being punished for it.

One Muslim creation story calls humankind the *caliph* of nature—the representative, the agent, the proxy of God. Humankind is charged with the care of creation according to the rules fixed by Allah. Allah remains the supreme ruler of creation.

The Judeo-Christian creation story tells of human beings created in the image of God. In that story they are not only capable of mastering the whole of nature, they are charged with that task. This story can be blamed for the aggressiveness of the Western approach to nature. *Thanks* to that story the syllabus on "environmental education" had to be introduced in East Africa.

OUR "TOLD" EXISTENCE

The stories we tell are of great importance to us. They help to shape the way in which we experience the world and our attitudes toward it. If that is so, we might ask ourselves, considering the sad state of affairs of the world around us, whether we are telling the right stories! Problems of war and peace, human relations in society and church, science and religion, capitalism and socialism— all are endlessly discussed in meetings and publications, without descending into the depths of our myths about origin and eschaton, about man and woman, about humanity and God.

We know (and experience) that our existence is sick and wrong (we know and experience this negative side more acutely than any positive side), but we rarely penetrate to the foundations, the roots of our "told" being. On the surface we are liberal, bourgeois, modern people. When we scratch that surface a bit, we find opinions and myths dating from a period that has been officially abolished and relinquished. Missionaries and evangelists have observed this in their African converts. Placide Tempels wrote about it in his book *Bantu Philosophy*:

Among our Bantu we see the *évolués*, the "civilized," even the Christians, return to their former ways of behavior whenever they are overtaken by moral lassitude, danger, or suffering. They do so because their ancestors left them *their practical* solution of the great problem of humanity, the problem of life and death, of salvation and destruction. The Bantu, only converted or civilized superficially, return at the instance of a determining force to the behavior atavistically dictated to them. Among the Bantu and, indeed, among all primitive peoples, life and death are the great apostles of fidelity to a magical view of life and of recourse to traditional magical practices.[1]

This text is riddled with colonialistic expressions. We can forgive this if we read the preceding paragraph in the same book, where Tempels writes similarly of the modernized European.

It has been often remarked that a European who has given up, during his life, all practice of the Christian religion, quickly returns to a Christian viewpoint when suffering or pain raises the problem of the preservation and survival, or the loss and destruction of his being. Many skeptics turn, in their last moments, to seek in the ancient Christian teaching [stories and myths] of the West, the *practical answer* to the problem of redemption and destruction. Suffering and death are ever the two great apostles who lead many wanderers in Europe at their last moments to our traditional Christian wisdom.[2]

Not only that type of crisis brings the old stories back to our minds. Isn't the old story about Noah and his sons the origin of the many modern white persons' and the Boers' attitude toward land and toward the "coloured" races?

BIBLICAL MYTHOLOGY

Some years ago the German-Canadian, Jesuit biblical scholar Fidelis Buck sparked spirited discussion at the University of Nairobi. He told his audience at a public lecture there that it would be good if the whole of the Bible would disappear from hearts and libraries, from minds and bookshelves. He exaggerated. His statement, however, was understandable in the fundamentalist circles where he was teaching as a guest lecturer.

The fundamentalist view incorporates these beliefs: God made creation out of nothing; angels and humanity resisted God; a flaming sword was used against the whole of humanity even before the first fratricide; the first murderer killed his brother after having been rejected by God; and woman (notwithstanding all modern demythologization) was formed out of man. It is a view that only can lead to a world full of contradiction and disaster. Under the influence of those tales our world is divided into a good camp and a bad camp; into those who are of God and those who are of the devil; into those who are allowed to collaborate and those who are going to be detained.

Several studies have been undertaken to consider theology after Auschwitz. However, few theologians really drew their theological conclusions from the holocaust. But can any theologians do that, given the biblical material they have at their disposal? Aren't the biblical myths the roots of those terrors?

This difficulty does not exist only in the stories of the Old Testament. We meet it too in the New Testament. It is, of course, a relief to learn that Paul was antifeminist only because the Canaanite religion against which he was reacting was full of suspicious goddesses, sacred prostitutes, and fertility cults. Yet what are we going to do with all those stories and myths that, notwithstanding the work of scholars and experts, continue to tell what they have always told over the centuries? Anyone who has ever been a pastor or a preacher knows how frustrating it is to explain a text by showing that it really does not say what it seems to say.

MISUNDERSTOOD

Biblical stories have been often misunderstood. They have been often misunderstood by spiritual leaders who did not always have the best of intentions.

The Dutch professor Krijn spent his whole professional career proving that the revenge-theme, preached by Saint Anselm and later canonized in church doctrine, is not to be found in the Bible.

According to Krijn, the Bible never says that Jesus carried the *punishment* for our sins or that he appeased God's *wrath*. Yet those ideas have determined, in the name of the Bible, the course of the lives of many. Those ideas have caused sincere Christians to speak of reckoning, penance, and punishment. In the secular realm, those ideas have influenced many modern non-Christians to speak of and act with revenge and hate.

Recent theological studies deal with "experience" and "contrast-experience." They tell us we should pay more attention to our contrast-experiences when we read biblical stories. We can't avoid telling stories. Even scientific and technological progress can only be integrated and tolerated in our lives through our stories. Don't we try to justify the arms race with reference to the myth about the struggle between us and "godless" communism?

We should tell new stories. How do we get them? At the beginning of this chapter we considered the experience of an interreligious contact in a Kenyan secondary school. The teacher of environmental education was confronted with three different mythologies that had had three different effects in their respective cultures. Would it not be possible to construct out of those three a new synthesis? Isn't that exactly what Africans are asking when they are confronted with Jesus Christ? Should we not have more interest in our interreligious contacts? Should we not be more attentive to the whole of all those varieties within the human religious heritage in order to do justice to our contemporary religious and moral needs?

17

Denominationalism and Religion

In 1969 the Kenyan scholar John Mbiti wrote his book *African Religions and Philosophy*.[1] A strange title with a plural and a singular. Mbiti intended something special with that title. He wanted to show that, although Africa counts as many religions as it does peoples, the fundamental attitude toward life is the same throughout Africa. This observation seems valid for the peoples in certain regions of Africa, even after their acceptance of the most varied forms of imported religions and ideologies. To the outsider it is often a total surprise to find—in a country like Kenya, for example—representatives of almost every possible expression of the Christian faith: Roman Catholics; members of the older Protestant churches; and followers of a wide range of denominations (including the fundamentalist ones from Holland and the United States) that have developed more recently within Protestantism—Quakers, Seventh Day Adventists, Jehovah's Witnesses, members of the Church of God, and so on. Some of those groups have more members in Kenya than they do in their countries of origin. Alongside those churches we find more or less Africanized forms of the Coptic Church, the Greek Orthodox Church, and the hundreds of Independent (often officially registered) Christian church communities.

In this respect Kenya differs from neighboring Tanzania. The number of Christian denominations is much smaller in Tanzania. Independent churches exist, but in comparison to Kenya their number is insignificant. Christianization began in Tanzania at about the same time as it did in Kenya. Its impact, however, was felt much earlier there than in Kenya. In Kenya the conversions began after the First World War, but did not really increase until after the Second World War. Then the struggle for political independence had begun and it influenced African Christianity.

The situation in Uganda is different than it is in Kenya and Tanzania. In Uganda two large Christian denominations, the Roman Catholic church and the Anglican church (later called the Church of Uganda), competed (sometimes violently—the first automatic rifle introduced in East Africa was used in the struggle) from the very beginning. The state of affairs was aggravated because the Catholic missionaries were French and the Protestant ones were English. Both Christian communities had difficulties with Islam. Although the leaders were at war, the faithful did not have the same difficulty. When the king of the Baganda decided to do away with his "converted" court pages who refused to obey him, Muslims, Protestants, and Catholics together suffered martyrdom for their faiths. Today, political divisions in Uganda run for the most part parallel religious divisions. Ugandans (and the missionaries) ask after elections: How many members of parliament are Catholics, how many Protestants, and how many Muslims?

Such a question would never be heard in Kenya because there are simply many more religious denominations in that country. In Kenya one finds Christian churches and the old Islamic coastal community; there are many adherents to Hinduism and Jainism; there are many members of other religious groups—the Hare Krishna, the Children of the Divine Light, the different Yoga groups, and the Kenya (not officially recognized) Moonies of the Unification Church; finally, between 30 and 40 percent of the population has remained faithful to its traditional beliefs.

NYAYO

Notwithstanding those religious differences, or maybe thanks to them, if Mbiti were to write a new book on the religious condition in Kenya, he could retain his original type of title. The title might be "African Religious Denominations and Philosophy," or, perhaps more to the point: "African Religious Denominationalism and Religion."

To the outsider it is confusing to see how Kenyans can switch from one religious celebration to another. In the case of mixed marriages, the changeover from one Christian denomination to another does not seem to offer the slightest problem. Africans go to the nearest church without paying much attention to the denomination that is meeting there. A Spanish priest was surprised to see one of his parishioners turn away from the Catholic church. The priest asked the man where he was going. The answer was: To that church there!" The parishioner pointed to a large church-tent put up by an American Baptist group. The priest asked in astonishment, "How can you do a thing like that?" The man answered, not knowing the consternation he was causing, "Your church is full; I don't like to stand outside; maybe there is still a place in that one."

This interdenominationalism is not only true of Christian services where Catholics and Mennonites, Methodists and Presbyterians are often piously worshipping together. Even Christians and Muslims sometimes come together. And in times of real crisis the old beliefs and customs are not forgotten.

Christians from Tanzania and Uganda are often horrified when confronted with the Kenyan situation. Some time ago the papers in Kenya announced that the Roman Catholic bishop of Nakuru was going to celebrate the Eucharist in the Anglican (Church of Kenya) cathedral. They said that it would be a "first." Later the announcement proved to be untrue. The bishop only preached in the Anglican cathedral. Many had come for the Mass. The fact that such an announcement could be made and believed is an indication of the nature of the Kenyan religious environment.

Jomo Kenyatta, the charismatic leader who led Kenya to its independence and who died as its president, participated in all kinds of different religious celebrations. One Sunday he went to an Evangelical Brotherhood church, another Sunday to the Catholic cathedral, another time to a Bahai meeting, and so on. In most places he was asked to say something. Kenyatta's preaching—always religious and political—made the same points. We are, notwithstanding our religious differences, all children of the same God, we are brothers and sisters and we should live accordingly in peace, love, and unity. He always added that we should forgive and forget whatever had happened in the past.

Kenyatta's successor, Daniel Arap Moi, developed a political philosophy called *nyayo*, "footsteps" (following in the footsteps of Kenyatta). Moi's message was like Kenyatta's: peace, love and unity. It is significant that in that slogan the word *justice* is not mentioned.

"SAVED"

Because of this religious intermingling many official ecclesiastical admonitions and warnings cannot be applied, especially when they come from Western countries, from totally different religious environments. Take, for instance, what Pope John Paul II used to say about the Christian (Catholic) family. The normal Kenyan family structure is, as far as religious affiliation is concerned, heterogeneous. The family situation reflects the situation in the country and vice versa. The mother might be a Presbyterian, the father a Methodist, some daughters Pentecostal, one son a Catholic, another son a Muslim, while their grandparents have not given up their traditional beliefs. What good are ecclesiastical directives in such a situation? The Kenyan bishops too come from this kind of background. The archbishop of Nairobi baptized his polygamous father on his deathbed. Another bishop has a Muslim brother.

Even under those circumstances, life—religious life—has to go on. The Africans have found two ways to survive in this religious maze. The first way is to apply a Christian formula of faith imported from the United States by the Baptist communities. It is a well-known formula: I am saved! In that confession of faith the whole creed is reduced to the individual, who declares: I accept Jesus as my personal Savior. The most important religious event is the witnessing to the "being saved" in fellowship meetings, which are organized again and again. It is possible in this way to escape from the existing religious confusion. Thrown back on yourself you are alone and do not have to bother about others. This solution, however, does not always work. Such persons remain interested in the others and their "salvation." They constantly bother others with the question: Are you saved? If those others do not understand that question, or if they do not want to listen to it, any relationship is usually broken off. The "saved ones" eat apart, separated from the others in the dining halls of most Kenyan colleges and universities. They try to avoid contact with the others as much as possible. They often do not even shake hands with them. They are the religious exceptions in Kenya.

UNIVERSALITY

The second way to survive has something to do with the title of Mbiti's book. It is a response more in line with what is happening in Kenya religiously. The Kenyans, who once all belonged to a traditionally religious group, have to leave many taboos and customs and practices behind when they become Christian or Muslim. They can make that step only if they are prepared and willing to consider those traditional religious particularities as unimportant, as mere details. Because African converts come from all kinds of traditionally religious peoples with different beliefs and practices, they also consider each other's customs as unimportant details.

This process, which all converts have to go through, makes things relative. Customs and rites that were once of vital importance prove unnecessary. A clear insight into what is essential and what is accidental, what is helpful to life and what is not, is thus created.

From this type of experience Kenyatta learned his universalistic approach to religion. It can be enlightening to look (again) at Jesus from this perspective. The fruitfulness of such a reconsideration was apparent in a recent discussion in Kenya's largest agricultural high school (Egerton College, Njoro). About five hundred students and staff had come together to discuss "the usefulness of religion in view of human welfare." The discussion began with the not-too-original remark that Jesus Christ was not Christian. But he was not a real Jew either, someone added. He was universal in his religion. His message was that we should behave justly toward each other; we should forget the past, be reconciled with each other, and live in justice and peace. During the discussion the Bible was often quoted, notwithstanding the presence of several Muslims.

Had Jesus not told the Samaritan woman who asked where God should be worshipped—in the temple or on the holy mountaintop—that the time would come when such a difference would not matter, and that people would, by that time, live in justice and truth? Did Jesus not stop the temple service in Jerusalem shouting "From now on all will worship me," to the great amazement of the Jews in that temple, who thought him a blasphemer? Did not Paul write to the Christians of Ephesus: "I am the apostle of the pagans. I have in fact only one thing to tell you. Up to now it was unknown. It was a secret. Now the secret has been revealed: *we are all one in Jesus.*"

The best argument put forward, however, was based upon passages in the Old Testament. Jesus used this same argument in Nazareth when he explained his intentions to the people in his hometown (see Lk 4:16–30; 2 Kgs 5). He told them that he had come to start the year of grace. They got very enthusiastic. He then explained that this year was for all. Before he had finished, their enthusiasm was gone.

To illustrate his point Jesus used the story of the widow from Sidonia and the story of Naaman. Naaman was the commander of the army of the king of Aram. The Aramaeans were traditional enemies of the Jews. They had won several battles against the Jews. Usually everyone in the losing camp was killed, men, women, and children. The only ones who were spared were the young maidens who were taken home to serve as house slaves.

Naaman had such a girl in his house. He became sick with leprosy. The Jewish girl told her mistress: "If only my master would approach the prophet of my country, he would be healed of his leprosy." Naaman's wife told him what the slave girl had said. He went to the king and asked for a leave of absence so that he could visit the prophet. The king said, "Go by all means. I will send a letter to the king of Israel." Naaman left bearing gold and silver and fine clothing as gifts. Instead of going to the prophet directly, he went first to the king of Israel who, to his horror, read in the letter his guest brought with him: "With this letter I am sending my servant Naaman to you for you to cure him of his leprosy." Somewhere the information had been wrong. The king of Israel did not know what to do with the letter, which should not have been addressed to him. He became very upset because he thought the king Aram was trying to find a new excuse for a war. He tore his garments and sat in sackcloth and ashes.

When the prophet Elisha heard about this, he sent word to the king: "Why did you tear your garments? Let him come to me and he will find there is a prophet in Israel." Naaman was sent to Elisha the prophet. When he arrived he did not get out of his chariot. The prophet, offering tit for tat, did not come out of his house. He sent a messenger to Naaman, saying: "Go and bathe seven times in the river Jordan and your skin will become clean once more." But Naaman was indignant and went off saying: "Here was I thinking that he surely would come out of his house and heal me. Why should I wash myself in the river Jordan? The rivers in my own country are definitely better than the water of that trickle in the sand." And he turned to go in a rage. But his servants told him: "Listen, if that prophet had asked you to do something difficult you surely would have done it. Now he asks you to do something very small and you don't do it." Naaman let himself be convinced. He washed in the Jordan and he was healed. He went back to the prophet. This time he got out of his chariot. He went to the prophet to thank him. He wanted to give him silver and gold, but the prophet would not accept it. Then Naaman said: "I have one further request. Please, hear me!" The prophet asked, "What is your request?" Naaman answered: "Give me as much earth from your land as two mules can carry, because your servant will no longer offer holocaust or sacrifice to any God except Yahweh." He was converted to the God who had healed him. But then he hesitated. Suddenly he understood the implications of his words. How would he be able to be faithful to what he promised? Being the commander-in-chief, he had to accompany the king when he went to sacrifice to the local god Rimmon. While he offered sacrifice, the king leaned his left arm on the right shoulder of his army commander. Naaman could not avoid that religious act without getting into serious trouble. So he explained his predicament to the prophet, concluding: "May Yahweh forgive your servant this act." And the prophet Elisha said: "Go in peace." It was almost as if he said: "So what? Go in peace."

In referring to Naaman, was Jesus indicating a difference between the *essentials* in a religion and the *details*? Was not his message essentially that all human beings, from whatever people, tribe, or sex, are one? Was not this the truth he lived in his life? Is not this the basis for any claim of justice for all? Was he not arrested, detained, tortured, and finally killed because of that insight? Did not God guarantee the truthfulness of Jesus' vision by raising him from the dead?

To the participants in that discussion it seemed that the followers of Jesus had gone wrong when they started a new group different from all the other groups in their world. It seemed they started by saying: "We are saved; we are of him and you are not."

NEW DEVELOPMENT

The discussion reminded me of a conversation I had with a student at the major seminary of Kenya. We were discussing whether the missionaries had brought anything new, really new, in their message. We suggested all kinds of "new" data. In each case the answer was: But our ancestors knew that already, but our ancestors believed that too. Then the idea of universality was mentioned. Was it not true that all the old values counted only within the context of one's own people? That idea of universality—that all human beings from whatever people form together the one family of God—was something new.

The veri-fication of that truth in the reality of our everyday life is the mission Jesus left to humanity. It is probably Jesus' last mission in this world. It should be obvious to anyone of good will that the fulfillment of that task is more possible and more necessary today than at any other moment of human history.

Nairobi, the capital of Kenya, is a very interesting place from the point of view of universality. It is a religious center. The World Council of Churches has its African headquarters in Nairobi and held its 1975 meeting there. Rome established its Institute of Higher Ecclesial Learning in Nairobi and several Protestant theological faculties are also located there. Nairobi was chosen as the site for the 1985 International Eucharistic Congress, the first held in Africa. It was no one's intention that Nairobi should become the center of Catholicism in East Africa. Nairobi should have become the African Geneva, and Kampala, the capital of Uganda, the African Rome. Because of developments in the latter country this became difficult. But Nairobi seems to have become both the African Rome and the African Geneva. One of the signs of our time?

18

Alternative Decision Making

A parish council was meeting somewhere in the center of Africa. That parish council had not been appointed by the bishop or the parish priest; it had been elected by the parishioners. The council numbered twelve members plus the parish priest and his assistant, who had come recently from Europe.

The issue under discussion was the admission of someone to baptism. It was a complicated and difficult case. The deliberations lasted a long time. The young assistant from the West became impatient. He looked at his watch. Finally he could not keep quiet any longer. He said: "If we go on in this way we are never going to end. This might go on for hours. We all know what we want. Let us take a vote. Who is in favor of his baptism and who is against? Let us decide by a show of hands."

It was as if someone had suddenly discovered a snake under the table. Everyone looked up, frightened. How could he propose a thing like that? Did he want to divide the parish council? The issue was the concern of everyone. Obviously in such a case the consensus of everyone was needed.

The chairman of the meeting said: "Many thanks for your suggestion. We are grateful for your contribution. There is someone else over there who would like to say something. . . ." The meeting continued until everyone agreed with everyone else. The baptism was postponed by unanimous decision. Before reaching that point of agreement everyone had to talk for a long time.

LIFE-ISSUE

A group of sociologists and psychologists from Scandanavia lived for some time with the Rendile, a nomadic people in northeastern Kenya. The Rendile still migrate with their camels and other animals from one grazing place to another. One of the issues the Scandinavian scientists wanted to study was Rendile decision making—when, how, and why does such a people at a certain moment decide to break camp and move on. Such decision is of vital importance to that people's life. If they make the wrong decision, they might perish.

The Scandinavians had to wait for weeks and weeks before they could start that part of their research. Finally the moment arrived. On a given night the people all came together. (The meetings were held at night because during the day everyone was out with the animals.) A man opened the consultation by making a proposal. Everyone listened until he had finished. Another spoke: "I agree fully with the first speaker. I think I cannot correct him. I admire his unequaled wisdom and his deep insight, but I would like to make just one additional remark." A third speaker took over. He praised the two preceding speakers. He said that he asked himself what he might be able to add. He too finally added his own suggestion. A fourth spoke, a fifth, a sixth one. Everybody agreed with everbody else. Each one, however, added a new element, a nuance, an amendment, all through the rest of the long, slow-moving deliberations. It would have been preposterous, unbecoming, almost indecent if anyone had exhausted the topic on his own.

The deliberations went on and on, all around the circle of participants until early in the morning. Even after everyone had spoken that first evening, no decision was made. They met a second night and a third until finally all had had their complete and exhaustive say, and all those words, affirming and complementing each other, had grown together into an organic unanimity. Everyone knew what, where, and when everything was to be done. The deliberations did not stop before everyone has made his contribution and before everyone was in agreement. If the decision reached in this way would prove to be wrong, nobody would be able to blame anyone else. There were no losers and no winners. The people would not be divided. It would not fall apart. Nobody would be able to say: "Didn't I tell you?" Under the circumstances in which those people lived, they could not afford the luxury of opposition or of a split. That would mean the end of the whole group.

DIALECTICS

Experts in Europe and America know now that Asian dialectics is different from the dialectics of the West. It is not as well known that in Africa too a different dialectics is used. It is even forgotten, it seems, by Africans educated in the West. A. Makarakiza, a bishop in Burundi, wrote in his book *La Dialectique de Barundi* that the logic used by his people is the same as that used in the West. That may be true. However, the dialectical process—within which the logic is applied—is different. That difference is obvious to any European or North American who ever participated in an African discussion. Because of this difference a student at the university or a worker in a factory asks permission for some days' leave when there is a "problem" at home. Problems demand time.

The word *no* is rarely used in African discussions. If it is used, it is not with the same meaning as in the West. If one would say during a deliberation, "I disagree completely with you. I could not disagree more, you are totally wrong," one would place oneself outside the circle. Any further discussion would be impossible. There is no further point of contact.

CONFLICT THEORY

Western dialectics is very old. Some of the earliest philosophers in the West felt that the idea of Thales of Milete (considered by many the first Western philosopher) that everything came from one element, water, was untenable. How could fire be reduced to water? "Reality," according to those early philosophers, grew out of the perpetual struggle between water and fire, a process that took place in something called *apeiron*, the qualities of which were undetermined. Heraclitus remarked that conflict is the parent of every thought and of all progress. The dialectics of Aristotle were based upon the opposition between affirmation and negation, act and potency.

In the nineteenth century, this type of dialectics was developed in the studies and writings of Hegel and Marx. According to them a *thesis* generates its *antithesis*. Out of their conflict a *synthesis* is born, which becomes in its turn a thesis, which generates its antithesis and a new conflict. According to Marx, conflict, class struggle, is a necessary element in human history. Fighting is what makes us "tick." Jean Paul Sartre illustrated these dialectics in his considerations on being and nonbeing. Being, he says, is dialectically based. One says: "I am who I am, because I am conscious of who I am and who is the other." The other is in that case not only my opposite. The other is my negation, hell. We in the West have become so accustomed to conflict that we even idealize it. The pacifist Jim Forest once wrote that he hoped that conflicts would be part of our lives in heaven. Without those conflicts, he thought, human life would be impossible. That was the exact opinion of Heraclitus.

We seem to need opposition. Without opposition we think we have no position. Thus we organized a society of conflict. Without a Protestant, there is no Catholic. Because of this prejudice Western observers judge the African one-party states (whether they are capitalist or socialist) to be undesirable, dictatorial, and even unbelievable.

DEMOCRACY

The Rendiles' point of view seems to be exactly the opposite. The Western multiparty system is dictatorial, because a majority rules over the rest. Within a multiparty system only the majority is taken into account. That majority forms one group. Such a division of power divides the population into different political factions. Persons and ideas are either this or that. They are either white or red. They are either capitalist or Marxist. Every problem becomes a party problem. Because of party politics the general welfare becomes secondary. When vital decisions have to be made, party politics cannot be trusted. The consequence is that the more important the issue is, the smaller is the group of those who decide. War and peace do not depend on the people but on the ruling individuals.

If the Rendile were divided into a ruling party and an opposition party, and if decisions would have to be made in that kind of system, their chance of survival would be slim. They cannot allow themselves such polarization. This does not mean that every one-party system in an African country is good. In fact many one-party systems are not good; they are dictatorial and have remained true to the old traditional ideal only in appearance. The fundamental condition that makes the system work is overlooked: each person does not listen and is not willing to listen to every other person. There is no dialogue.

In the West we must ask whether we can allow ourselves the luxury of "democracy." The ever-growing polarization is a threat to all of us. Our inability to sit down and talk with each other might bring about our end. The lack of dialogue is the main reason that our world is filled with threatening warheads and missiles. It is one of the reasons that so many of us feel powerless against the accelerating arms race. World political leaders speak in terms of East-West and North-South divisions and conflicts—divisions that can only lead to disaster. Would it not be appropriate to try another type of decision making? Could we not learn from the traditions of so many African peoples who have had the time to talk themselves out of problems and conflicts? Would all this not be applicable also to the community we call church?

19

Without Father

Every Christmas night all over Kenya, and probably all over East Africa, thousands of mothers go with their children to midnight Mass. They go in groups for safety against the dangers of the dark. They take care that some people are left at home to guard their property. The men do not come in the same numbers as the women.

Christmas is the great day, the greatest feast day of the year. The people go to visit the mother with her child. They go to visit the family that lived on the border between the old and the new, the transition family, consisting of Mary, and her child Jesus, and Joseph, a kind of godfather.

Michael Singleton contributed to a study published by the Belgian Catholic Information Service to assist the bishops in their preparation for their synod on family life. Singleton remarked that it is strange to venerate the family in Nazareth as the Christian community's model family. The family in Nazareth was fatherless, and the mother, Mary, had only one child. We all know, of course, about the special circumstances of that family. Yet, according to the faith of many, the family in Nazareth was a mother-child unit. What did Jesus answer, when somebody asked him: Who is your father?

A social worker asked the children in one of the heavily populated quarters of Nairobi the same question. She asked: "Who is your father?" It was not the most tactful of questions. Almost all of the children answered: "*Hayuko*," which means "He is not here."

According to official statistics, 65 to 80 percent of all those mothers who go to celebrate Christmas will do so without husbands. In almost all those families the woman carries the full burden of her household. This is often because her husband works far from home. In a growing number of cases it is because the women in the urban areas and upcountry do not wish to marry. "Children, yes; a husband, never," is the feeling of an increasing number of women. If you ask their reasons, they are quite willing to tell you. They want to spend their own money. They like to decide themselves about the use of their bodies. They do not want to risk marrying a man who may turn out to be a drunkard and who might not care about the rest of the family.

Sociologist Kenneth Little noted in his book *African Women in Town*[1] that a new type of African family is emerging, a family consisting of a mother with her children, children born of different men. This does not mean that those mothers have no other relatives. These fatherless family units are usually connected with the extended family of the mother. Did not Mary, once pregnant, visit her relative Elizabeth? A detail like that does not escape the attention of the African Christian.

SURVIVAL PATTERN

Sociologist Elizabeth Colson wrote an article entitled "Family Change in Contemporary Africa" for the book *Black Africa: Its People and Its Culture Today*.[2] She noted that this change in the structure of the family unit is not restricted to urban areas but can also be found in rural regions. It seems to be due to the marginalization of the men. The men have lost their traditional roles. Traditionally they educated the boys who had reached puberty; they protected the hearths against animals and enemies; they hunted and fished for food. The schools have taken over the education of the boys; the police and the army have taken over the protection of the homesteads; and hunting (often fishing too) is forbidden. The men, having nothing to do at home, leave to look for work. Work is hard to find. When it is found, it is often a type of work that does not give the men their traditional dignity. They become house servants or workers in a textile factory, doing the things traditionally done by the women.

The research of Dr. Judith Bahemuka Mbula in Kenya showed that the wives, and even the children, do not see any function for their husbands and fathers in society. The men are of the same opinion. They are needed less and less; they drink more and more. The saying of the women—"children, yes; a husband, never"—has nothing to do with amorality or immorality. It has everything to do with the survival pattern of the people. Notwithstanding these difficulties, the Africans have great respect for fertility and for God's gift to humanity, human life. The difficulties are due to the frightening economic difficulties of the people. Those difficulties are related to global injustices in the world.

At the synod on the family (1980), Bishop de Jong from Zambia expressed his fear that the existence of the African family is in danger. He noted:

> Many of the problems facing families and family morality in the developing countries are not isolated ones. The underlying causes must be sought in the situation of misery and oppression in which families, especially the poor, find themselves. This situation is a direct result of *global injustice* inflicted on the poor of the earth.[3]

Archbishop Daniel of Pretoria, speaking in the name of the South African Episcopal Conference, said that industrialization and urbanization have not only destroyed traditional cultural values in many parts of Africa, but have also made a normal family life impossible.

> The process of urbanization, with its attendant problem of inadequate accommodation, is forcing African families into—at best—the nuclear family situation. I say "at best" because in many cases even the nuclear family cannot exist. With industrial development, unskilled workers were forced or drawn out of the reserves to earn a meager livelihood in mines, factories, and commercial enterprises, or as domestic servants. This migratory labor system completely disrupts family life and strikes at the very roots of family stability. It produces "single married men" and "single married women," with the resulting mistrust of each other, and fatherless children at home.

The changeover to urban conditions deprives the family of the protection formerly enjoyed in the traditional environment and often creates an educational vacuum which has devastating effects on family life and results in premarital sex, teenage pregnancy, single-parent families, and divorce. Consequently some children roaming the streets of the ghettoes do not know either father or mother, or family in the formal sense.

In many cases, because of low wages, young people cannot meet the demands of the "bride price," with the result that couples live together for years and have several children without going through any form of marriage, tribal, civil, or ecclesiastical. Moreover, the appalling social and economic conditions and the insecurity in which so many urban Africans have to live result in innumerable loose, irregular unions.[4]

Africans know that they are in a transitional stage. This means, in everyday life, that they are aware that it is impossible to be faithful to the old and that it is difficult to know what exactly to do. Church legislation is no solution. Few Christian Africans marry in church. The number of those who do is decreasing. The marriages that take place in church are usually between older men and women who have been living together almost all their lives. In some parish registers, "ill." is entered after the name of every child, meaning "illegitimate."

All those women and children go on Christmas to honor the child Jesus, born from Mary, a girl of about sixteen years who, according to the gospel story, herself decided to become a mother. It is as if they go to encourage that mother and as if they themselves want to be encouraged in their situation, which none of them considers to be ideal but which allows human life to continue.

There is something special about Mary's child. In many African societies the child has hardly any status. It achieves status as it grows up and passes through each initiation stage. A child is never asked for advice or for an opinion. It is taken care of, but nobody expects anything from it. It still has to be socialized, and its status will grow as it is introduced into the society of the adults. The older, the wiser; the older, the more honored. This is the normal pattern in traditional societies.

But the pattern has changed. Modern Western culture reaches the children before it reaches the older members of society. The roles are reversed. Children are telling their parents: "You never had any education." According to a study of Professor Philip Mbithi, chairman of the Department of Sociology at Nairobi University, children are now educating their parents.[5] It is comical and at the same time distressing to see young volunteers straight from European or American colleges instructing and advising older and wiser Africans on agriculture, cattle breeding, housing, health, and even family planning.

The students of the national African universities are educating their elders too. Because their learning is from books, the students often look down upon anything traditionally African. Mbithi notes that this is not only true of university and college students. Even primary school children tell their parents that they are wrong, old-fashioned, or that they do not solve their problems well. And the parents keep their mouths closed so as not to seem foolish in the eyes of their own children.

Salvation will come from new input, those parents seem to think. Salvation comes from the children. Salvation will be the gift of the Christmas child. All those mothers on their way to worship that child are full of hope and expectation. They fervently hope that in the midst of the African night, in the midst of the falling apart of civilizations that have sustained African life for tens of thousands of years, a new light will shine—a new light from God, a new beginning.

The priests of the diocese of Nairobi came together for a pastoral council at a beach on the Indian Ocean at Mombasa. They decided to do their pastoral work under the motto "compassion." That word *compassion* does not only mean *pity*; it also means *understanding*. Is it, however, really possible for those priests to be compassionate and effective within existing church structures? Would it be possible to allow all those thousands of mothers to receive communion on Christmas night? Would it be feasible to create a church in which all those African Christians who are struggling with problems that are not of their own making can be guided without constant reference to an alien model, that of the classical Christian Western family? At the moment that model clearly is impracticable and of no help to them.

At the Roman synod the African bishops spoke about various types of marriages. They spoke of marriages that are validated at the birth of a first child (and sometimes only after the birth of a first son). Those bishops spoke almost exclusively about *marriage* and hardly ever about the *family*. It was as if they did not want to touch the difficulties of the family.

The women, the children, and the men walk through the East African night toward churches where midnight Mass will be celebrated. They all want to celebrate Christmas—the birth of a child, born of an unmarried mother, as some modern children's Bibles say. They will jostle around the cradle to see the child, the savior of the world. They will go home hoping that in the end all will be well, hoping that their own condition will be understood and forgiven by that child.

20

Science and Religion

The letter came from Europe in response to an article. The reaction did not come from a stranger; it came from a good friend. The letter was short. There were no opening words, no greetings. The name and address of the sender were typed. There was no signature. The content of the note does not matter. The content was not the difficulty. The difficulty was the tone. After a polite but thorough complaint was sent in response to the letter, a more personal letter was sent from Europe. There was even an apology. The apology stated that the author of the letter had not taken into account that he was writing to Africa. He added (he had lived in Africa for several years) that he had forgotten that there everything is personal. Here in Europe, he wrote, we are businesslike.

The first carriers of the Christian culture into Africa were the missionaries and evangelists. They did not only bring the gospel. They brought much more. They built the first schools. They started the first Western clinics and hospitals. The missionaries brought practically the whole of Western science and technology, including all the assumptions of those disciplines. Almost all African leaders began their scientific careers in missionary schools. They do not forget that. Even when they no longer consider themselves Christians, they never forget to thank the missionaries for what they brought.

In his book *The Missions on Trial*,[1] Walbert Bühlmann describes a fictitious trial in which missionaries are accused by the Organization of African Unity of having brought to Africa more chaos than order. The defenders of the missionaries plead their cause by making two points: the missionaries were the first to bring education to Africa; they were the first to bring medical assistance. We are accustomed to this. We expect missionaries to be involved in human development. But there is a difficulty.

The missionaries brought Jesus. They baptized in his name. They told the people that Jesus was a life-giver. They repeated what Jesus had said about himself: I came to give life, life abundantly. They brought that life, however, in two different forms: religious and scientific. The mystical and sacramental life was in their churches; the material and concrete life was in their schools and hospitals. It was absolutely new to the Africans to separate those two. In their experience those two aspects of human life had always been so intimately connected that a separation seemed impossible. Many African languages do not even have a special term for "religion" or "worship." Some older Africans therefore maintain that religion and worship were imported by European missionaries.

In the Independent Christian communities each worship service includes a healing session. Direct results are expected during the prayers over the sick and the possessed. Help comes, not in the hospitals and clinics, but within the praying community. This is perhaps the reason that the relation of science to religion is one of the most popular topics at secondary schools and colleges.

Most missionaries admit that they did not arrive in a religious vacuum when they came to Africa. The missionaries found a religious world; they did not introduce religious attitudes. But those same missionaries will say that they introduced schooling, education, and medical care to Africa. It seems to them that the Africans had not done anything in those fields. That is not true, but the misunderstanding still exists.

Missionaries only gradually became tolerant of African religions. They eventually came to appreciate African customs and values. They understood that Jesus Christ should become God-man within the African context. Pope Paul VI approved that kind of incarnational theology years ago when he visited Uganda— though when he later met in synods with the African bishops he had some difficulties with the practical applications of those principles.

When it comes to the Western scientific vision, this tolerant attitude seems to be missing. The Western scientific way of thinking—the Western rationalistic, objectivistic, materialistic approach in the fields of medicine, physics, chemistry, and biology—is for the most part intolerant of alternative African attitudes toward science.

A similar situation exists in the West. Parents in Europe and the United States can decide what kind of religion their children are to be taught, or whether their children are to be taught any religion at all. This is usually not the case when it comes to the teaching of science. There is little or no choice. Basically, only one scientific attitude and method are taught. To pass examinations and advance academically or professionally, students must concentrate upon that method and attitude, to the exclusion of other perspectives. The children are free to believe in God or not, but they have to believe in scientific concepts that were almost all developed in the West. They have to think in terms of atoms, molecules, neutrons, protons, electromagnetic fields, and so on. Science does not allow an alternative. But alternatives do exist.

ALTERNATIVE SCIENCE

An example of the value of a scientific alternative can be found in the case of China. The West once colonized that enormous country in the usual way. Western religion and science were introduced and imposed. Existing scientific methods and skills were pushed aside. In 1933 the Chinese scholar Chou San wrote: "What corresponds to Western science may remain living, what does not correspond with it should die."[2] Chinese doctors were not allowed to treat patients in the old ways. The use of herbs and acupuncture were considered things of the past and no longer seriously studied.

That attitude prevailed until 1954 when Mao Tse-tung ordered the universities to study Chinese medicine as well as Western medicine. Traditional Chinese medicine became known in the West and now is often used to heal the sick after Western methods have failed. Not only do Chinese and Western medicine differ in method and approach. Another difference lies deeper—a difference in world vision. This cannot be explained in a few words.

It is not the topic of this book, but it might be useful here to say something about it.

Aristotle observed that the first question of the Greek philosophers was: What are things made of. According to Empedocles water, fire, earth, and air were the four constitutive elements. If you were sick, something was wrong with your physical or chemical constitution. If you had a fever, you had too much of the element fire, which could be extinguished with water. If you had a cold, you were too wet, and a bit of fever would dry you up. This approach, though more refined, is evident even today. The Western medical approach to sickness is to either add or subtract one or another element. A powder or a pill, an injection of a suppository is applied to restore a healthy chemical balance.

In the Chinese world vision, the first philosophical question was of a different sort. The Chinese started from the idea that everything had an inner law, a blueprint, a life-law, an inner melody. They called that element *tao*. Their first question was: How do I live in harmony with my *tao*? The art of human life was, according to the Chinese, to discover your inner melody, the hymn you were supposed to sing in life, and to sing it as well as possible, in harmony with nature. In the Chinese vision, sickness is not a lack of some "thing"; it is a lack of inner harmony, an unequal division of energy in one's being. That lack of harmony can be restored by acupuncture or by heating one or another part of the body.

THE AFRICAN ALTERNATIVE

The first African question is (according to most experts): How can *we* survive and prosper in *our situation*? The important thing is that human *we*, which should relate to surrounding nature in such a way that human life can continue and prosper. That *we* is not only restricted to the human community. It includes all that is necessary for the human community to survive—plants, animals, and minerals, all that has been given with human life. Life in its totality came from God, the great common ancestor, and life continues to flow from him. Probably because of this attitude, the first Western travelers to Africa thought that to the Africans reality was animated. These discoverers called African belief by many names: animism, fetishism, totemism, or magic. They put all of these under the category "religious attitudes" and considered them to be pagan or superstitious. Some missionaries said that the African vision could have come only from the devil, and in certain cases they even added that Africans were so black because they had been sitting so long, not in God's sun, but in the shadow and smoke of hell.

For the African, sickness is a relational problem. One is sick because one does not relate well to one's neighbor, to the community, to nature, or to God. African doctors try to know as much as possible about their patients. They try, sometimes in very dramatic ways, to restore appropriate relations. In other words African doctors have always been aware of the psychosomatic aspect of human sickness.

This does not mean that no medicines are used. Herbs are important in African medicine. Herbs are plants in which God has obviously put special life-powers. They can stimulate and heal human life because of those powers. Western doctors too admit that herbs can be effective, but they view the function of herbs in a different way. A Dutch doctor in a popular book *Modern medisch advies* (Modern medical advice) wrote:

> Herbs have no medical significance anymore. All the chemicals that are useful in plants are known and can be chemically prepared. Medicine can not and may not rely anymore on the uncontrollable substances and quantities of herbpreparations. Medicinal herbs are for amateurs, not for patients.[3]

This opinion excludes the possibility that those plants in their organic wholeness, in their life-force, have a healing power.

Sometimes Western researchers find out about one or another herb used by a traditional healer against a sickness. Not so long ago it was discovered that bark from a certain bush was used successfully against cancer. Westerners in such a case would cut down a whole grove of those bushes, strip off all the bark, and ship it to an overseas laboratory for analysis in order to isolate the active, healing ingredient and to manufacture it synthetically.

THINGS FALL APART

Only recently has the African world vision been studied seriously. In 1967 Robin Horton, a philosopher who had worked for several years in West Africa, observed that the African vision, in which humankind is surrounded by personified forces, is not just a religious belief but a scientific explanation of the behavior of nature.[4] This statement seemed nonsensical to many European scientists. Western scholars think not only that their approach to science is correct, but also that it is the only possible scientific approach. Reality can, according to them, only be understood by way of the Western "thing-models"—a misconception that prevailed even after scientists had discovered that this model had to be complemented by wave and electromagnetic-field theories.

Africans and Westerners essentially had the same reason for developing their scientific theories. All were confronted with the same problem: a reality they did not understand. They did not even understand themselves. Direct insight was impossible. Reality could only be reached and "explained" via examples, thought-models. It was not only a question of understanding the working of nature. They wanted to understand in order to be able to foretell, to master, to use, and to manipulate.

The Greeks chose *things* as their thinking-models; the Africans chose personified forces or "spirits." Horton explains why those different choices were made. In trying to explain the regularities in nature, both groups chose as their model the most reliably behaving item they could think of. For the African that item was the human person in his or her behavior in community. The Africans lived in communities where human behavior was strictly organized. The behavior of the individual was predictable. The Greeks were urbanized by the time they developed their science. They had lost contact with the more traditional human community structures. The behavior of the Greek townsperson was unpredictable. The Greeks consequently chose another model. The things that surrounded them were more predictable. Therefore they chose things, atoms.

The scientific and the religious approach are integrated in the

African vision of reality. Scientific explanations are in line with religious beliefs. In the West that integration gradually lessened. Separation even became an ideal. In 1648, when the first association of scientists in England, the Royal Society, was set up, its constitution made it clear that science would be fostered without consideration of "divinity," metaphysics, morals, politics, grammar, rhetoric, or logic. Theology was separated from science, religion from the rest of life.

This segregated and secularized Western science proved to be very effective. It was effective because it worked with only part of the data of human experience. The Western vision was successful because it was simplistic. Western discussions about science and scientific developments bespoke this attitude: Let us not think too much about the consequences, especially the moral consequences of our scientific progress. Let us go ahead. Come on, let us go ahead!

Because of its success, the thing-model became a model for all of what we might call the natural sciences. Karl Marx used that model to understand the human community and its history. Even in theology, grace was considered to be a *thing* you either had or did not have, and the idea of a living relation with God fell away to a great extent. Pierre Teilhard de Chardin speaks, notwithstanding his grand and organic vision, about human persons as "little things," "particles," and about human minds as "little grains," "granules."

The existential philosophers, theologians, and novelists reacted against this thing-approach. Their warnings have not to be repeated here. Their philosophy has a great attraction for African students. The Africans know well how degrading it is to be considered a numbered thing, a unit, in our modern world.

Within an African vision, the Western scientific view of reality seems strange, even incomprehensible. Africans simply do not understand how it is possible to reduce the whole mysterious reality to which we all belong to a thing or a set of things. African students who are confronted with this type of explanation cannot believe it, though they have to in school. That "having to believe" often leads to enormous tensions. The African tries to solve the problem by saying, "I can believe all this as long as I am at the university or in school, but when I am at home with my family, I don't believe it at all.''

AN ALTERNATIVE

Missionaries to Africa unknowingly introduced the existing schizophrenic situation. Bühlmann suggests that the missionaries uprooted African culture only by the introduction of Western Christianity, but not by the introduction of Western scientific medicine and education. I believe he is mistaken. The hospital and the school did more to break down traditional African values than the church did. The juxtaposition of science and religion meant the end of the African vision.

The fault, if we can speak of fault, is not only on the side of scientists. The Christian churches also carry a great responsibility. Church leaders and theologians had little interest in engaging with scientists in dialogue. That such a dialogue is necessary is obvious if the African point of view is considered. How to begin that exchange is a difficult problem. A first condition is for theologians to criticize themselves. To what extent have they allowed objectifying tendencies to penetrate their theories? We need a theology that will be able to heal humankind. Africans always expected their religion to heal. In the beginning of this century the pragmatic philosopher and psychologist of religion William James wrote:

> Thus the divorce between scientific facts and religious facts may not be as eternal as it at first sight seems, nor the personalism and romanticism of the world, as they appeared to primitive thinking, be matters so irrevocably outgrown. The final human opinion may, in short, in some manner now impossible to foresee, revert to the more personal style, just as one path of progress may follow a spiral rather than a straight line. If this were so, the rigorously impersonal view of science might one day appear as having been a temporarily useful eccentricity rather than the definitively triumphant position which the sectarian scientist at present so confidently announces it to be.[5]

Elsewhere in the same book James remarked:

> When from our present advanced standpoint we look back upon past stages of human thought, we are amazed that a universe which appears to us so vast and mysterious a complication, should ever have seemed to anyone so little and plain a *thing*. There is nothing in the spirit and principles of science that need hinder science from dealing successfully with a world in which personal forces are the starting point of new effects.[6]

James hoped for an alternative, a new approach. He hoped that humanity would return to a more person-oriented world vision. Perhaps a study of the African vision could help bring science and religion together.

21

A World Falling Apart

The hall was full. The listeners were so numerous they had invaded the stage and were sitting behind the participants in the forum. Tension was high in the hall. A hush followed the eager applause that greeted the speakers.

When a group of students in East Africa is asked to determine the topics for a series of extracurricular lectures, almost invariably one of the topics will be "Science and Religion." Students and teachers of all levels will come again and again to hear lectures about subjects such as "Evolution and Creation," "Faith and Modern Science," or "Is God a Scientist?"

Some feel the reason for this interest is that the African intellectual is living in a Victorian or even a pre-Victorian age. Some say that what is happening now in Africa happened a century ago in Europe and America. Only now are modern science and modern techniques infringing on traditional belief-systems in Africa; only now is this profoundly "sacralized" world being confronted with a "secularized" or "scientized" alternative. Those persons suggest that the difficulty will gradually disappear and they prophesy that secularization will win out.

The issue is much discussed among African scholars. John Mbiti's view is most popular. He holds that Africans are essentially so religious that they will remain faithful to their religious selves through all the ages to come. Scholars like Okot Bitek hold an opposing minority view: the religiosity of the African is nothing but an invention of the invading missionaries from the

West. According to Bitek, African life and culture were essentially humanistic, attempting to make human life and survival possible in harsh and bitter physical environments.

Against this background we will examine the difficulties Africans have when they try to combine their religiosity and modern science. In this almost uninvestigated area it is impossible to be complete or completely accurate, but some tentative remarks seem nevertheless to be justifiable.

In commenting on African religious attitudes today we should keep in mind that generally the first Christian missionaries did not appreciate the African religious and moral situation they found. In some cases the missionary church, together with the colonial government, actually intended to destroy African religious and moral practices. In many cases this process alienated the Africans from their own religious heritage. While this was occurring, two new alternatives were offered simultaneously to the Africans.

The first of these alternatives was Christianity. The second was introduced by Christianity: the educational, medical, and technological approach of the secularized and scientific West. In a sense the missionaries represented two streams of thought, two beliefs: belief in Jesus Christ, his mission, and his church; and belief in the efficiency and "goodness" of Western technical know-how.

Those two "beliefs" were not integrated. They were separate, and that is what upset the African value-system, in which religion and all aspects of daily human life—birth, health, sickness, and death—were interwoven.

Christianity presented itself as redemptive and life-giving. Jesus Christ himself thus described his mission: "I came to bring you life, life to the full!" But it was in the scientific field that this new life-power from the West seemed most evident. It was through science that people healed and acquired new skills and techniques. It became quite a problem—deciding which belief to accept—especially as the two were not integrated in the way that all dimensions of human life were integrated in most African worldviews.

THE THING-MODEL

Another difficulty contributed to the problem. Western scientists usually interpret natural phenomena according to a thing-model. Reality is explained in terms of atoms and other sub-atomic "things." It is often forgotten that those "things" are only thought-models, that they are means of conceiving of reality but are not reality itself.

As mentioned in the previous chapter, in Africa the thing-model seems never to have been used to interpret natural phenomena. Africans interpreted reality in terms of personified forces. When confronted with this African "scientific" interpretation of reality via the model of personified forces, Western scholars considered it to have no scientific value and relegated it to the quaint African religious world vision. Western scholars failed to understand that the African thought-model was indeed a religioscientific explanation of reality; they disqualified it as mere religious superstition. In one sweeping and erroneous judgment they did away with the African's scientific *and* religious outlook. African religion and African science were disqualified.

Africans were supposed to start from scratch. They tried to blot out everything they thought, experienced, or believed before. Their only help lay in the alien religious and scientific ideas imported from the West. Thus many Africans today are alienated from their roots. Although research into traditional African morality and philosophy is far from complete, one thing seems to be obvious: the original African moral and philosophical system was centered on *human life*.

A Western thinker would probably have no serious difficulties with this philosophy in theory. However, in order to practice this philosophy Westerners would have to radically reorient themselves toward the world and others. In today's capitalistic, mercurial, and consumer society, profit, production, and consumption seem more important than anything else, human life included. This materialistic view of life, preached in advertisements, bombard the African day and night. The armaments race, the development of the neutron bomb, and the daily exploitation of human life to insure profit are all indications of the turn Western society seems to have taken, a turn setting it in opposition to the more traditional ways of life.

The "development" introduced from the West is usually confined to the material areas of life. Religious and moral values are generally overlooked, except in those fortunately frequent cases in which the church, in its community building, manages to keep body and soul, world and human, human and God together.

THE ALTERNATIVES

The general devaluation of the African traditional system, which has been caused by both expatriates and Africans, has created a vacuum in the lives of many Africans. This vacuum will be filled, but Africans will have to choose how to fill it.

They could return to their traditional system. Every African country has its believers in a back-to-the-old-heritage movement. It is unlikely that the old traditions can satisfy the modern African. African tradition as such is probably not viable in the modern world.

They might try a complete surrender to Western science and technology. The danger here comes not so much from science and technology as such, but from the problems that arise when one tries in daily life to put into practice a materialistic worldview that ignores transcendent and moral values.

They might try to fill the vacuum by an exclusive reliance on the new religion offered in the Bible (or for Muslims in the Koran). A fundamentalist attitude characterizes many of the hundreds of the independent churches in Africa. The number of these groups of the "saved"—saved from the world, from history, and from material development—is growing rapidly. But this human reductionism of reality will not be satisfactory either, except perhaps in cases where the human situation is temporarily desperate.

The Africans might try another approach, a more integrated approach.

SACRED WORLD

According to the deeply religious orientation of the African, human life is God's greatest gift to this earth. Because of this insight, the theory of evolution is difficult to accept and creates many problems in the African context. Africans want to believe that they come straight out of God's hand, and they are worried about the slowness of the evolutionary process and the possibility that such a theory could be used to classify people according to norms of apartheid.

The African orientation—which is based on the religious and mystical insight that human life and the quality of that human life in all its aspects is the most important issue—should be preserved and developed in the context of the proclamation of the life and teaching of Jesus Christ. The human person alive is the honor of God our Father. The Father's restoration of human life in its fullness through Jesus Christ is the heart of the good news. Material development and technology should be integrated into this mystical, moral vision of reality. Science should be "sacralized," not in its methods but in its aims and intentions.

The impact of the Western world on Africa threatens to alienate Africans from their fundamental and original religious, moral, and scientific experience. The danger is that the vacuum created will be filled either by a one-sided Westernized science and a materialistic lifestyle, or by a fundamentalist, antiscientific, escapist "religious" attitude.

The possibility also exists that within the complicated African context a new lifestyle can be created in the light of the personality of Jesus Christ—a lifestyle in which the human relationship to God and to the world is integrated in such a way that God's greatest gift to this world, human life, may come to its fullness. This fullness will be the best possible worship. In this way the African problem of relating science and religion will be solved. Africa's solution may be a God-given opportunity for the whole of humankind.

22

Pain and Suffering

The man was bitten by a mosquito. He was quietly asleep early in the morning when a mosquito entered his room through a crack in the wall. That mosquito could have picked another crack in another room. It did not. It chose this crack, this room. At first, it had some difficulty orienting itself in the partially dark room. Finally the mosquito fixed itself on an unprotected piece of human skin. It pumped some fluid into that arm to be able to suck better. The pumping-in was worse than the sucking-out. Malaria parasites were deposited in the blood of the man, and within a few days he was very sick. He went to a doctor, who explained to him the whole story about the mosquito bite. When the story was over, the patient asked the doctor: "But why did that mosquito come to *me*? Why to *me*? What would be the reason for that?"

If that patient had gone to a traditional African doctor, the doctor too would have asked that question. Most probably he would have found the answer. Why did that mosquito bite that man and not another one? This story has been told so often that it is like an old joke. But John Mbiti, in his book *African Religions and Philosophy*, discusses it in a serious way.

COMMUNITY THEORY

To ask why that mosquito flew to one particular man and not to another one indicates the belief that the bite and consequent sickness are symbols or signs of a deeper meaning. The sickness was in

143

some way intended—by someone who wished the patient evil or by some other person, thing, or force. One thing is sure: anyone who gets sick has something in his life that is not good. There must have been something wrong in his relationships with his fellow human beings, with his ancestors, or with nature. Sickness is a sign of that—not a punishment, but a warning, a sign.

Consequently the doctor's task is not finished when he has prescribed the appropriate medicine. He is supposed to do and to know more. He should not only combat the symptoms; he should also go to the root cause of the sickness itself, physiologically, psychologically, and morally. That holds true not only for individual, personal disease. It also holds true when a whole community is threatened by a contagious disease, for example, or by any other disaster. In fact, it is difficult to speak of a purely personal disease in a tightly knit community. Everything is so interconnected that the sickness of one is seen as a sign for the whole village.

The doctor and the assistants act as spies or informers, trying to find out as much as possible about what has happened to the sick person. They analyze the patient's family life; they investigate old, forgotten quarrels; they study the sick person's relationships with the dead (who never died completely). The social and economic status of the patient is thoroughly investigated.

Some people, like the Acholi, organized annual or biannual meetings with the whole community, during which the doctors (Okot Bitek calls them diviners) did their healing.[1] Those doctors not only cured physical ailments by administering medicines; they also dealt with the psychological problems of their patients. Medicines made of herbs, plants, powders, seeds, roots, juices, leaves, bones, minerals, and ashes restored disturbed relationships and harmonies.

Okot tells how the sick persons were sometimes put in a kind of pen that would be surrounded by the healthy people. The doctor would dance around the patients, and using the information he and his assistants had obtained, he would hint to both parties where things had gone wrong, where relationships had gone awry. He would remind them of unresolved quarrels and of hidden feelings of revenge. He would sing about guilt and fear, about jealousy and hatred. In other words he would try to provoke a kind of catharsis, allowing everyone to go home relieved and liberated. Some sacrifices would be offered. Guilt would be spit out. In some cases preventive "medical" measures would be prescribed: a taboo would be declared, some types of food would be forbidden. The prescription might even be to avoid a certain person.

This kind of procedure could lead to serious malpractices. That possibility, however, also exists in the Western approach to medicine. In a Western context abuse might be even easier than in a situation where the whole population is involved in the healing process.

ILL HEALTH AND RELIGION

In the garden of an old Salzburg family guests from all over the world were gathered. They had come to Salzburg to celebrate the Salzburger Festspielwoche, an annual event honoring one of the most famous sons of the town, Mozart. Many of the guests also participated in the Theological Hochschulwoche, organized annually to run concurrently with the musical event.

In the group was a doctor, a pediatrician. He mentioned that he had worked in Africa. Someone asked him if he had learned anything in Africa, if his stay had been useful to his career. He answered emphatically: "Of course." He told them that when he first arrived in Africa, if a sick child were brought to him, he would treat only the child. He had done that because of his Western training, but it did not help. African mothers did not seem to trust his methods. They looked at him with pity in their eyes. He had asked his African assistant; "What is the matter; is there something I do wrong?" The assistant had looked at him to check the sincerity of his question, and then she had told him. The African mothers were telling each other that he could heal European diseases but not the African ones. They had told the assistant herself that he did not understand a thing about sick African children. He asked her how they had gotten that extraordinary idea. She answered: "You never give any medicine to the mothers of those sick children, but only to their children." He had answered: "The mothers are not sick!" She had laughed loudly. "That is exactly the point," she had told him. "How could a child be sick without there being something wrong with the mother?'' From that moment onward the doctor always treated mother *and* child. Back in Salzburg, he continued that practice—with great success.

Generally the concept of ill health in Africa is different from the concept of ill health in the West. Okot Bitek suggested in a speech given at the University of Nairobi in 1971:

> What is the concept of ''ill health'' to the African in the countryside? The medical student ought to try to get an answer to this question. He must learn about witchcraft, about the vengeance ghost, about the cult of ancestors. The study of African religions ought to be made compulsory at medical schools. What do you do when your patient complains of a splitting headache, and adds that he has been bewitched by his neighbors? How do you handle the case of someone who believes that it is the ghost of her mother who is troubling her? Medical students should turn their attention to the works of the diviners. Our medical schools ought not only to carry out researches on the medicines used by the diviners, they must also do serious studies on the African concepts of ill health; and the study of African religions forms the core of this work.[2]

No wonder that Mbiti wrote that in the African context sickness and disaster are religious phenomena. Sickness indicates difficulty in communicating with God. Disease is a sign that something somewhere went wrong. Isn't that the idea we see in Jesus' actions as told in the Gospels? Didn't Jesus connect sickness, dumbness, blindness, paralysis, and leprosy with sin and guilt? Didn't he often begin his healing processes by saying: ''Your sins are forgiven''?

Healing cannot be worked out only by medicines or messages. Healing has something to do with God. In the independent church groups, healings are an important part of worship. A group of African theologians and pastors who came together in 1978 in Yaoundé, Cameroon, recommended the following:

> Let us work at the mission Jesus gave us: preaching, teaching, baptizing and *healing*. Let us do whatever we can to

heal the sick in hospitals, at home, and in the traditional ways of healing; let us appeal to our Christians to act as "healers." Let our pastors help in hospitals; let us develop our charismatic healing gifts; let us pay more attention to our prayers for the sick, and the sacrament of the sick.

More than a hundred pastors from all over Africa signed the recommendation, which ended with the observation: "This concerns all ministers!"[3]

SICKNESS AS SIGN

Not only the fact of sickness is a sign. The nature of a sickness is also a sign. Emaciation indicates a shortage; a swelling indicates a superfluity. The disease is a sign of two problems. An intolerable headache not only indicates something wrong in the head of the sufferer, it also indicates that something is wrong in the community where this headache originated. Personal pain not only functions as a distress signal for the sufferer, but also for the whole community. Sicknesses are signs on the wall written by God's hand.

Over the past years Western doctors have become aware of what they call the psychosomatic aspect of human disease. Stomach and duodenal ulcers are often caused by "undigested" feelings of guilt or fear. These types of sicknesses are typically human diseases (though it seems that certain young animals can develop a stomach ulcer if they are not accepted by their mother). So in the West the medical profession is becoming (again) aware of the connection between sickness and human relations. Disease has something to do with morality. This connection makes sickness into a sign, even within a secularized society. In a religious context such a sign is seen as *prophetic*.

SICKNESS AND MYSTICISM

All through the ages "saints" have considered their pain and their suffering as signs of the unhealthy situation in which society tries to survive. Some of these saints became well known. Francis of Assisi had wounds in his hands, his feet, and his side. Toward the end of his life, it was said that the skin of his face became rough and painful because of his weeping over the state of the world. There are others who are less well known. Liduina of Schiedam in Holland; Benedict Labré, who allowed himself to be eaten by lice and fleas under the walls of the rich and pompous Vatican in the name of the kingdom to come; Charles de Foucauld; and the controversial Padre Pio of our day.

One of these lesser known "saints" was Edith May Barfoot. She lived from November 28, 1887, to April 30, 1975. From the age of sixteen, she suffered from rheumatoid arthritis. Eventually she was unable to walk. In 1960 she became blind and, some years after that, deaf. She suffered very much. In 1928 a priest asked her to give him some notes on suffering to help him to prepare a retreat. Edith complied. Her notes, entitled *The Joyful Vocation to Suffering* were first published anonymously in 1928.

She wrote that she understood herself to be a God-sent sign to the people around her. She saw herself standing in Jesus' place after his scourging when Pilate said "Ecce Homo." Pilate was not saying this of Jesus only, but of every human being, of our *human condition.*

Even before they knew about Jesus Christ, Africans seem to have looked upon disease and suffering in a way that was similar to the perspective of Jesus and those saints. Pain and suffering were signs, warnings: we should readjust our lifestyle; we should drink, eat, or smoke less; we should take more (or less) physical exercise. When our total human body—humanity, society—is sick, we will feel pain. Some parts of our common body will start to signal us to stop, change, reorganize, convert, correct, amend!

DENIAL OF SUFFERING AND PAIN

As long as our world is not the kingdom of God, there will be suffering and pain. As long as the significance of these signs of our incompleteness is suppressed, we will continue to suffer. As long as humanity is unwilling to accept its groanings and pains, indicative of the new humanity that will be born, that birth is delayed. If suffering and pain are indicators of the fact that our world is not well organized, then those who profit from the existing structures will be unwilling to recognize those signs. Recognition would mean change. The easy way out is not to see the signs, to oppress and suppress them. We do not want to see the sick and suffering around us. They should not be part of our world, so we isolate them and lock them up far away from us. The world's avoidance of suffering and refusal of pain are signs of its unwillingness to change, to convert.

It should not be forgotten, however, that pain and sickness are never desirable in themselves. Edith Barfoot wrote:

> Having made the surrender to the call it is at times fatally easy to lose heart and sit down, making no effort to go on trying to better one's condition. This attitude of mind is entirely wrong and contrary to the will of God. When the soul realizes this challenge in the call she should be filled with enthusiasm to do her level best to accept the assistance held out to her by the science of medicine and surgery in the effort to better her physical condition. She must be a fellow worker with all those who try to help in the struggle, even though it may appear that such help is of little or no avail. She must not let discouragement or frustration break down the will to struggle and to try again and again, even when it be with "grief and pain."[4]

After we accept our suffering as a sign of what is wrong with the world, our attempt to be healed is a further sign of what the world should desire to do. With God's help we are bound to be successful in the end.

MALIGNANT TUMOR

Western culture sickness is personal, individual. It would be strange in Europe or America for a sick person to go to a doctor together with his or her whole family. In another culture such a visit to the doctor would not be strange. People of those cultures do not understand the Western bourgeois interpretation of sickness. To them sickness is not only seen as something of the community, it is also seen as a sign to the whole community.

Sicknesses come and go. It might be possible to write a history of diseases. Some sicknesses occur in one period, others in another. A historian could write the history of a sickness taking into account only chemical and physical factors. Some cancers, for example, may be caused by our use of plastics and other artificial substances. Not long ago a Western-trained African doctor gave a different explanation of the causes of cancer. He described cancer as a growth that is no longer under the control of the central nervous system. He called that central nervous system the "central life force." An organism suddenly starts to develop independently of all other organs in the body, without any relationship to them. It grows and grows, oppressing and suppressing all the rest, forgetting it has not even a good reason for existence on its own. "That is what happens in those patients," the doctor said. "That is what is happening to our world," he added, "not only in Africa, where a few are getting immensely rich at the cost of the suffering of others, but also in the rest of the world, where the North has grown inordinately wealthy at the cost of the misery of the South. That is cancer too, a malignant tumor."

23

Non-Bourgeois Theology

The so-called "undeveloped" groups, those groups that have had little or no contact with Western development, are a delicate subject of discussion in East Africa. Masai country is a mere thirty miles from Nairobi. In Masai country one can see giraffes and waterbucks on their way to a watering place in the evening.

The Masai living in the region are faithful to their old traditions. The young warriors walk around with ocre-colored patterns painted all over their bodies, a sepia mixture in their hair; they wear a free-flowing, stone-red, one-piece garment. To the irritation of the national leaders they do not wear trousers. They are armed to insure the protection of their wives, their children, and their herds. They eat their traditional diet of milk and cow's blood. In their idle moments they can stand endlessly on one leg, looking over the immense plains. What is to be done with this group of people who are not willing to betray the lifestyle that has guaranteed their survival over thousands and thousands of years? What is to be done with them in a world in which almost all other peoples have already betrayed their traditional lifestyles?

University professors started the discussion. Okot Bitek argued that lifestyles like that of the Masai should be kept intact. Others were of the opinion that the Masai should be involved in the national development programs and that they should start to "work." Economists wanted to divide the Masai's land and then convert them into settled farmers.

The discussion spread among the students. In a tutorial on the topic of culture, one student said that he thought those idle people should be put to work. Another student became very angry at that. He said that all the Masai participate in their community. It was nonsense to say that they were not working. Everyone has a place, a role. Sitting around the campfire in the evening, everybody in the group counts. No one is frustrated. Everything holds together. That was not even the most remarkable thing, he said. There was something else besides. He then compared the Masai situation to the situation in the West. He asked: "How many people count in the West? How many of them feel part and parcel of their societies? Who knows in those societies about the political decisions? Who knows why there is a war, or why there is peace? Who knows what is happening and how it is happening? How many do not simply say 'it is the system' when they send their children into their disastrous educational system?" Answering his own questions, he added: "I think not even two million people rule the West. The rest do not count. They do not know anything. They are only an obstacle to those two million, puppets in their hands. Is that the pattern we want?"

He went on to explain that the Masai would lose their dignity, just as almost all the others had before, that their morale and their morality would collapse, that they would all try to take refuge in one or another church. Instead of their own educational system of initiations and rites, they would have to go to an alien and alienating school; instead of their own judiciary system, exercised by the elders who know the people individually, they would get justice administered by foreigners who know nothing about Masai customs; instead of healing the "whole" of the sick among them, they would get chemical treatment for some organs in their bodies; instead of their own equitable distribution of food and goods, others would come in with their money-making markets and shops; instead of their integrated religion, they would get a Sunday-celebration in a church run by exotic religious professionals.

IMPOSITIONS

"The leading circles in Europe imposed their own forms on European society, and went on to impose them on the whole world.'''[1] This statement was not made about theology, but about philosophy, and is contained in *A Concise History of Philosophy*, written by Bernard Delfgaauw, a Dutch philosopher. This book was used by the students of the University of Nairobi as a text-book. The students had sufficient experience to know the truth of the second part of the statement. They were amazed at the first part. So in Europe too the *common* man and woman had been oppressed. Western philosophy was the philosophy of a certain group, and it was imposed upon the minds and hearts of the rest.

Confronted with the possibility of an African philosophy, many of those students were even more amazed. The leading participants in the discussion simply stated that there is no African philosophy. That is to say, there never was any African philosophy until some "Westernized" African scholars started to discuss Western philosophy in the Western way.

P. J. Hountoundji is the most outspoken representative of this point of view—a point of view held by almost all of Hountoundji's African colleagues at Nairobi University.[2] He states that one can speak of philosophy only when written documents and formalized discussions on the topic exist. This means that there was no African philosophy before Hountoundji and his colleagues started to write on philosophy. There is a good reason that this idea is widely held. The reason is that it is difficult to compare the formalized Western philosophy found in the works of philosophers like Plato, Aristotle, Hegel, Kant, and Marx with the philosophy of Africa, which is expressed in the oral traditions of the African peoples. Hountoundji and company maintain that as a part of the study of philosophy in the West people do not go to interview their grandfathers and grandmothers. Why, then, would people do that when studying philosophy in Africa? There is some truth in that argument (though philosophical interests in the West have been changing over the past decades), but ultimately the argument restricts philosophy to being an ideology of the leading class, as Delfgaauw noted in his book.

The argument completely overlooks the foundation of every philosophical activity. The general tendencies, the different "moods" of philosophy in the varied human cultures, were formed long before any formal philosophical argument was written down. Western philosophy began before Plato and Aristotle;

it began even before the pre-Socratics wrote down their first reflections. The trend of the pre-Socratics' philosophical approach must have developed over many years in the hearts and minds of the people in that culturally fruitful corner of the Mediterranean area.

Furthermore, how could one say that to be a philosopher one must write, when the man who was the turning point in Western philosophy, Socrates, never wrote down a single word? The formal statements of Indian philosophy written down in the Vedic manuscripts rest on thousands and thousands of years of previous development and maturation in oral form. Chinese philosophy was already ancient when Lao-tse and Kung Fu-tse worked it out in their writings. During the periods in which these philosophies were written down, "leading circles" formed, and often took over, forcing their own worldview on others. Those others had their own philosophy, their own reasoned and justifiable outlook in life. Of course there was an African philosophy before Hountoundji wrote. In fact some of his writings show his insights to be based on unwritten, oral African philosophy.

THEOLOGY

The same kind of argument can be applied to African theology. Here too we might restrict ourselves to formal, written work, and exclude the theological value of unwritten experience and insights. However, not only in Africa but also in the West this approach implies that the majority of believers do not have any valid theology. When we think of Western theology, names like Schillebeeckx, Küng, Barth, Rahner, and Tillich come to our minds. We hardly ever think of the millions and millions of people all over the world whose religious experiences are for them as valid and as authentic as Schillebeeckx's religious experiences are to him. It is odd that someone like Schillebeeckx puts an enormous amount of effort into study and writing on what common people in the early days of the Christian community experienced but does not seem to have that same interest for the common people of his own time.

At this point we must distinguish between Theology and theology. We must distinguish between bourgeois and non-bourgeois theology. To do this it is necessary to take into consideration the context in which the theologians live, breathe, and theologize. The distinction between the two theologies is real. It is a fact.

Before we make that distinction, however, we have to face a complication. A theologian is someone who studies and is interested in the human religious experience. Even the fact that the study of that experience is called *theology*, that is, the knowledge (*logos*) of God (*theos*), is an indication that the term was coined in the context of a certain *type* of religious experience. In other words, the term *theology* itself interprets the religious experience. Thus we encounter another assumption that prevents theologians from considering an experience like the African religious experience as a *locus theologicus*.

When a religious experience is interpreted in the study called *Theology*, the interpretation must, in one way or another, correspond to that experience. This is a complicated way of saying that a theological interpretation will be given when God plays an important role in an experience. Does God play an important role in all religious experiences? Does a religious experience occur only when there is an ecstatic encounter with the wholly Other?

In the introduction to his book *Ritual Cosmos*, Evan M. Zuesse makes some pertinent remarks on this issue.[3] He points out that the "leading theoretician of the academic study of religion, Rudolf Otto" describes religion and religious experience in the following terms:

> When the utterly transcendental "Holy" is experienced, the worshipper is overwhelmed with trembling awe and involuntary fascination. He is often ecstatically beyond time and space, and is unconscious of all else. The "savage" cannot interpret such terrific experiences correctly, but rather interprets the Wholly Other as demonic ghosts or witchcraft, developing propitiatory or magical rites to contain or to apply the sacred. (Only Christianity, Otto shamelessly insists, and in Christianity only Lutheran thought, understands the Holy correctly.)[4]

It might be useful at this point to consider the reaction of the East Africans in Rabai to the first Lutheran church service in their region. After the service they told the two Lutheran pastors that Africans did not worship in that way, and they explained that in their worship they ate, drank, sang, danced, and celebrated human life. They told those missionaries that in their religion, matters like human and natural fertility, social harmony, and everyday issues formed the content of their worship. Their view was very different from the Western view, where spirituality often means personal salvation from the "banalities" of everyday life. What should be done with African religion, which has such explicit emphasis on everyday life and its concerns? What should be done with a religion that does not make a split between the profane and the holy, and that consequently does not offer a power base for an exclusive priesthood?

NO RELIGIOUS MARGIN

That discussion between a few East Africans and the Lutheran pastors took place in front of a church building. The building, erected by the Lutherans, stood in an area where people once had worshipped in the open—under a tree, in a field, in a clearing in the forest. As long as people worship in nature, they can easily see that nature and human life are holy in all their aspects. As soon as a church or a temple is built, radical change takes place. The religious dimension is separated from the rest of life, caught and imprisoned in place and time. After this segregation nature and the rest of human life are viewed as profane. After this secularization of the world and life, religion becomes an extra, something at the margin of life, a super-addition, something supernatural. At that point priests begin to represent the other world that they themselves create—a world they will safeguard and defend, by hook, crook, and law, as their exclusive prerogative. Then the science of religion becomes the Theology of God in Otto's sense.

This conflicting "development" is not new in human history, not even in the history of the Bible. The deacon Stephen, in front of his Jewish judges, accused King David himself of having made the same kind of separation (Acts 7:44–51). David built a temple and everything changed.

Preparations for the 1979–83 development plan in Kenya included research into the priorities of traditionally living upcountry communities. The commissioners wanted to pinpoint the highest priority in such a community. Many were surprised by the findings. In most cases, priority number one was building a church. A cattle dip, a school, or a dispensary were lesser priorities. Why they opted for a church building first was not asked directly, but some "circumstantial evidence" made clear the reason for their choice. They needed the church building to be able to participate, after the segregation of the religious dimension from the rest of their life, in the Western *pagan* type of education, science, technology, medicine, administration, business, and even politics. The unresolved and omnipresent tensions in Western Christian culture—between theology and science, religion and politics, worship and human life—became blatantly conflictive in Africa.

Life lost its unity. Life lost its cohesion. Human beings turned against nature. One person turned against another within the same community. Elements of life were isolated from each other and became threats. Theology became the prerogative of a few and was often used to protect the principles and welfare of the few. The religious experience of the community was no longer the object of community study. Theology became scholarly, solid in its content, but also abstract. That high degree of abstraction has many advantages. Some of those advantages, however, are gained at the expense of losing contact with the everyday human life the believers live. The abstraction, though academically— maybe—necessary, is part of the cause of the dichotomy. The churches slowly were filled with middle-class people who were willing to rely on the priests, and the priests, in their turn, were willing to live on the people.

In the meantime hundreds of independent church groups started to meet in the open on Sundays—under the trees, in the parks, in front of urban shopping centers, and in the streets. With their liturgies, hymns, and theologies, they tried to bring things together again in a sometimes desperate effort to survive:

> They came together in their white long dresses, in their green and blue uniforms, above them their flags with the cross, stars, the sun and the moon blowing in the wind. The African Christians dance and sing, they speak in languages, and

experience a community that breaks through their tribal barriers, together with Jesus Christ in peace and security.

The missionary churches had not been able to offer the people these experiences, notwithstanding all efforts to make the churches indigenous and to put off their Western garb. But the real cause for the formation of the independent churches lies deeper. That cause is the African holistic approach to life. The Western churches tried to help the whole person with their schools, clinics, and agricultural programs next to their church buildings. But the separation in place and time remained strange to the African Christian. For them everything belongs together in the worship of God, in the worship of human life. That is why healing takes place during the service and at Easter some agricultural know-how is "preached."[5]

24

Worshipping Development

In the last week of June 1983, forty lay workers and some priests met at the Kanamai Conference Center near Mombasa. Most of them were members of diocesan development departments. They had been called together for what was to be the last time by the interdiocesan Christian Development Education Service (CDES). It was for the last time because the patrons of the service, the Catholic Episcopal Conference of Kenya, had decided to end the work of the CDES. The bishops had decided that the team was no longer necessary, that its services could be taken over by the national Kenya Catholic Secretariat. This decision had come unexpectedly.

The CDES had existed for over seven years. The seventh year, a sabbath year, had been devoted to a major evaluation of its work. The evaluation had been done in view of future activities, and now there would be no future activities. The CDES program of conscientization had helped hundreds of groups and thousands of people at the grassroots level to understand the structures that threatened their survival. The Masai knew they were going to lose their land; farmers were aware of the influence of international agribusiness run by Western multinationals; city-dwellers had a clear view of the injustices that caused the misery in the slums, and so on. Several members of the CDES team had been subjected to house searches, and some of them had been held by the police for a period of time.

During the meeting, the diocesan development education programmers, who were going to continue work within their diocesan structures, reported on their activities. The list of those church development projects was long and revealing. It was not a list of retreats or Bible study classes or pastoral seminars or prayer groups. It was a list that ran from water projects to the building of one-room houses for the disabled, from intensive-agriculture projects to literacy programs, from management and leadership courses for women to demonstrations on the use of semiarid land.

The participants in the meeting had many complaints, not only about the bishops, who were going to close the central service that had been running over the past seven years, but also about those who should have been directly concerned about CDES work in the field—the parish clergy. Many priests, in some regions more than 75 percent, had informed the CDES that they were not going to cooperate with the group because its programs were too materialistic.

Most of the participants in the meeting felt that there were a significant number of people who agreed with the priests' criticism of the CDES. However, none of the CDES team members had any difficulty in seeing their programs as work directly related to the kingdom of God. In their evaluation they even had tried to find out why they thought so. It had been one of their concerns. A whole chapter in their evaluation had been entitled "Christian Witness." They had tried to evaluate how far Christ's option for the poor and his interest in justice for all had been their motivating force. They had tried to measure how their work related to their life of prayer. They had come to the conclusion that direct biblical inspiration for their program was lacking. It troubled them that in answering the question "What was your main source of inspiration?", only 7 percent of the respondents had indicated the Bible, while 32 percent had answered "the needs and problems of the community," and 30 percent had answered: "our faith and our culture." The team members expressed the same concerns about the grassroot groups they had been leading that the priests had voiced. Were those groups sufficiently "spiritual"? Were they too materialistic? The team members formulated their concerns as follows:

Bible Studies and Prayer Life. The extent of biblical study and the use of prayer within Development Education Programme (DEP) groups were taken as the indicators of spiritual nourishment and guidance within the programme.

Although the Bible is one of the main guides for Christian living in the church and a source of motivation and inspiration for all Christian believers, this fundamental spiritual resource is not well integrated into the life of the DEP groups. Sixty-two percent of the sampled grassroots groups reported that they do not have regular Bible study. As shown by the following selection from their comments, the 38 percent which do Bible study have found it of considerable benefit.

"Bible study has strengthened unity and kept the members committed."

"The Bible gives members more courage and strength to do their daily activities."

"It has influenced the life of the group very much because those who were not Christians are now good Christians."

"Bible study has helped the poor because people who had no houses or clothes have got them from their groups and community."

The neglect of Bible study is a cause for serious concern, both because of the religious enrichment it can bring to the members and the groups, and for the maintenance of the DEP as an active Christian community. Prayer life is a demonstration of religious faith, the desire to maintain a vital spiritual link with God. In contrast to their use of the Bible, almost all groups (99 percent) reported that they prayed in all their meetings, mainly using the traditional Catholic church prayers such as the "Our Father," the "Hail Mary," "Glory Be to the Father," etc. Only one of the groups stated that its members prayed spontaneously, linking their expressions with the needs and problems of individuals, the community and the nation. Certainly spontaneous prayers such as these (or reflections on traditional prayers) would help to better integrate the life of the

Spirit and the struggle for earthly transformation within the DEP.[1]

"RELIGIOUS" MOTIVATION

Notwithstanding their doubts and hesitations, all the CDES team members felt they were religiously motivated. Where did that motivation originate if it came from neither their life of prayer nor their Bible studies? It definitely did not come from the church's preaching and guidance. Church practices had not even been mentioned in the responses, although all the respondents were church workers and churchgoers.

How was it then to be explained that they organized such a variety of activities from within a religious and church context? They had difficulty answering that question. Maybe the church wasn't the appropriate context for such activities. It seemed, though they hardly liked to admit it, that those bishops and priests who considered their activities too profane, too materialistic, not typical church work, might be right. But there was another set of statistics that seemed to indicate to them that they had not been too "horizontal" in their approach. Ninety-three percent of the educated people the CDES members had reached in their programs believed that God demands justice to be done here on earth and that God should not be seen only as a provider of justice in heaven; 59 percent also stated that the church should change its attitude and show greater interest in justice and peace issues, should encourage more lay involvement, and should opt more clearly for the poor.

Thus there were many people, besides the CDES team members, who were in favor of a Christian struggle for justice on earth. But what was the source of all that commitment to human-life issues within the church and Christian context? If it did not come from their prayers, or from their Bible studies, or from the church's preaching, where did it come from?

Deliberations on the topic lasted a long time. First there were discussions within diocesan groups; then the participants came together to exchange views; and finally a theologian reflected upon the issue. During that reflection it was suggested that because the participants' motivation did not come from the Bible, nor from prayer, nor from the preaching of the church, it came from a deeper level of inspiration—*from a level where they intuited that the real religious issue is human life.* "When life comes from God it is something divine," one participant remarked. "Worshipping divinity among us means taking care of and celebrating that unique gift from God." Another team member reminded the others of Julius Nyerere, one of Africa's Christian leaders, who once wrote: "We say man was created in the image of God. I refuse to imagine a God who is miserable, poor, ignorant, superstitious, fearful, oppressed and wretched."[2] On another occasion Nyerere said, "If a human being is really the temple of God, we have to do something about the flies in the eyes of a child, as those flies are ruining God's temple."[3] Still another participant commented that Jesus often worshipped God by healing *human beings.* When Jesus met a sick person, a blind man, or a bleeding woman, he would often say before healing the patient, "It is *in you* that I am going to glorify God!"

To worship God is to take care of human life, to enjoy and celebrate that life, to help and comfort it whenever it is frustrated, sick, or thwarted. Slowly it began to dawn upon the participants that their motivation had come more from their cultural heritage than from any consequent inspiration. But they also understood that one aspect of their motivation did not have its roots in their cultural heritage, and that aspect was their concept of *the extent of human life.* Julius Nyerere, *as an African,* wanted to be faithful to the traditional values that made his people unified, socially responsible, noncompetitive; *as a Christian* he wanted to extend those values to the whole of his nation, to all its people, and finally to the whole of the world.

The participants agreed that justice should be done to everyone. They agreed that the human rights of everyone should be respected. After much reflection they finally realized that the reason that justice should be done and that human rights should be respected is found in the deep, primary, fundamental insight that our human life is God's gift, is divine.

In one of its preparatory meetings, the provisory staff of the new Catholic Institute for Higher Ecclesiastical Studies in Nairobi was discussing its syllabus. One of the Ugandan professors proposed his syllabus on African spirituality. He proposed topics such as the spirituality of African experiences of polygamy. Though the group consisted mainly of East Africans, some Europeans, also future staff members, were present. One of them, an Italian, said: "I am surprised that in your course on African contemporary spirituality there is no mention of the justice issue. Should this not be mentioned in our Third World context?" The reaction of the African lecturers in the group was startling. They said: "No, that is not the primary issue with us. Our real difficulty is in the cultural field. Once our cultural heritage is accepted and digested, justice and human rights will follow."

It has been noted several times in regard to meetings sponsored by the World Council of Churches that the character of those meetings depends on the majority group. When the majority of the participants comes from Latin America, the main issue is *justice*; when the majority comes from Asia, the main issue is *religiosity*; when the main group comes from Africa, it is *culture*. Many of the African theologians who joined the first Third World theologians' conference in Dar es Salaam did not sign the final document of that conference because they felt that their experience was different from the Latin American liberation theology expressed in the final resolutions. For similar reasons Bishop Ndingi from Kenya did not want to call the small Christian communities in East Africa "basic Christian communities," the name used in Latin America. The small Christian communities came forth from a different experience, one not comparable to the experience that had given birth to the basic Christian communities in Latin America. The experience Bishop Ndingi noted was the experience of the African people. This was the experience the Christian Development Education Service had been trying to tap during its seven years of existence. The CDES had worked according to a principle formulated by a wise philosopher, Laotse:

> Go to the people
> learn from them,
> live with them,
> love them,
> start with what they know,
> build with what they have.
> But of the best leaders,

when the job is done,
when the task is accomplished,
the people will all say:
"We have done it ourselves."

This is the rationale with which the CDES ended its final report. In principle even popes agree with it. When Pius XII defined, in the required and solemn *ex cathedra* form, the last officially declared dogma on the assumption of Mary into heaven, he applied an age-old principle: "After having consulted the cardinals, the archbishops and bishops, who consulted their priests, who in their turn consulted the faithful, we are now in the position to declare. . . ." When it comes, however, to more familiar issues, like marriage or family and social life, even popes seem not to trust this approach. They will warn and threaten, as Pope John Paul II did in Nicaragua, that it might indicate a movement signifying that "the church is born rather from society than from the free and unsolicited initiative of God."

The application of the rationale that the decision-making process should occur at the grassroots level had led the CDES into difficulties. It had turned the CDES developmental programming completely around. Instead of having diocesan developmental authorities determine what was needed, the program had enabled the people to find out for themselves what they needed to do. No answers were ever given to questions that were not asked. The agenda came from the grassroots, and from the real questions of life.

This meant that the check and control had slipped away from the authorities. The paternalistic approach had given way to management by laypeople who consulted and cooperated with those who needed development most—the poor. That method had been the strength of the CDES in the dioceses where it had been working. It has also been, in a sense, its weakness. Here too the civil authorities had become suspicious because of popular awareness created by the service's conscientization programs. The church authorities became weary and wary of the CDES position. That is why the authorities opted for centralization and conformity when confronted with impulses from "below." The CDES was closed down and asked to regroup under the central, bureaucratic control of the Catholic Secretariat.

25

Prayer as Power

Thika is an industrial satellite-town of Nairobi. It is a town full of extensions of multinational corporations, and consequently it is a town full of rural immigrants. These immigrants felt the need to form small communities. The groups had to remain small, if only because of the limited space in the one-room houses where they met. A meeting could never consist of more than about twenty people. A good indicator that a group was getting too big was the breaking of the beds. If the group grew too big, the beds in the meeting room would break under the weight of the members sitting on them.

Because the groups were formed spontaneously, they were very different in character. They could be divided according to different criteria. One classification might be the way in which the members pray. Some of the groups are more traditional than others. The word *traditional* is of course ambiguous in an African Christian context. Here we mean it in the Christian sense. The more traditionally oriented small Christian communities say "set" prayers. They say the rosary together because some of their members are accustomed to that or once belonged to the Legion of Mary. Other groups are more traditional in the African sense. Their prayers are spontaneous; they do not use a set text. In their prayers they concentrate on their daily worries. The local, expatriate pastor expressed in several published articles that he, though a trained priest, learned to pray in the second type of community—the group that prayed spontaneously. He even said that he never really had prayed before. That might have been an exaggeration. It is, however, definitely true that in those small Christian communities the type of prayer that was practiced had much to do with determining the members' attitudes toward life.

PRAYERS OF THE FAITHFUL

Since liturgical reform began under Pope Paul VI, an official place has been given to the prayers of the faithful during the celebration of the Eucharist. Immediately after the Creed, just before the offering of the gifts, the priest invites faithful to come forward with their prayers. This hardly ever happens. Since the introduction of those prayers all kinds of liturgical writers have been providing priests with readymade prayers. Priests rarely risk opening these prayers to the people in the church. Their reasons are not difficult to guess. One never knows what those faithful are going to pray for. The embarrassment might be too great. It is safer to give the answer before the question is known. Isn't Christ the answer to all questions?

This domestication of prayer happens not only within the ecclesial family, where missals, missalettes, booklets, prayerbooks, and hymnals stifle spontaneous, and, in a sense, all prayer. It also takes place in the family. It is safer to pray a rosary together than to allow the family members to express themselves spontaneously. When father prays that Johnny will stop lying, Johnny might pray: "Almighty God, please take care that fathers drink less."

Somewhere in Masailand a priest was leading a liturgical service. He was "saying" a Mass in the presence of a mixed group of people—mixed in terms of sex, age, and level of initiation into Western liturgical Christian practices. An old man stood up. He interrupted the priest and said, nicely but insistently: "You have prayed. I heard you. Now I would like to pray, so that you hear me." The priest could not do anything but sit down and listen. Priests do not always do this. Even the pope does not like to be interrupted by people expressing in their prayers their real concerns. The ecclesial liturgical management will quickly intone a Te Deum, or a Magnificat. No manipulated prayer is ever charismatic.

CHARISMATIC PRAYER

There are stories that around 1916 a man in Rungwe, Tanzania, was suddenly caught from within by the Holy Spirit. Sometime later Alfayo Odongo had a similar experience in Kenya. The experience was common by 1926 or 1927, and was found simultaneously in Ruanda, Uganda, and Kenya. It is difficult to describe what precisely happened. The experience is difficult to capture in theological terminology.

Arthur Chilson was a missionary, a Quaker. He worked in one of the western provinces of Kenya in a place called Kaimosi. He asked a group of schoolboys whether they were really Christians. "You are not Christians at all," he told them, "nor are your parents!" The students were amazed. Some of their parents were even church elders. They asked him what they should do about it, and he proposed a weekend retreat in Kaimosi Forest. He asked them to confess their sins so that they should be totally open to the Holy Spirit. They had hardly even heard about the Spirit.

Suddenly it happened. It was like a new Pentecost. The boys started to speak in languages they had never used and never heard before. That was not even their most striking experience. They noticed that *they* were inspired from *within themselves*—not the missionaries, not the evangelists, not the expatriates, but they themselves. The time of spiritual alienation was over.

Some months later the same thing happened in a larger and an older group of persons at the Annual General Meeting of the Quakers. Sins were confessed, quarrelers reconciled, stolen goods returned, the sick healed, and the people spoke in tongues. Several participants felt themselves called to be prophets and preachers. They left the group and started new ministries. The official church leaders did not know what to do. They issued excommunications, prohibitions to preach, and took all kinds of other measures.

When things had cooled down a bit, it became obvious that this *Roho-Christianity* (*Roho* is the Swahili word for Spirit) would not go away. It was a different type of Christianity. The difference was that what had been coming from *outside* the people up to that moment now suddenly came from *within* themselves. The Spirit was a reality that started to work in the people. The

Spirit's activity was experienced by them as a sign in which God gave recognition to their own spirituality. They were confirmed by God as mature, adult.

It must have been a terrific experience for them. We should not forget that the Africans had been developing a spiritual inferiority complex. That complex was the result of much of the official church preaching. Before Africans were allowed to be baptized, they were sometimes obliged to attend catechism classes for three to five years. They had to abandon practically all of their own religious heritage. They were to start from scratch. But now the possibility of an independent church movement opened up. In no time, hundreds, and soon thousands of independent churches began holding services. One source reported that "during the past two decades 40,000 Christian Church movements have formed."[1]

Services are not held without leadership, but the leadership does not take all the initiative. The leaders ask, in an introductory hymn, that the Holy Spirit descend upon all present. A reading from the Bible follows. It is applied to the situation of the worshippers. Drums begin to beat, and off they go all together, singing, clapping, dancing. Just as it all seems about to get out of hand, the leader intervenes, stops the singing and the dancing, and slowly everything returns to "normal." A survey attempting to find the reason for the success of these almost endless services, found that the participants often said: "This is the only place where we are really respected. It is the only occasion when we are treated like human beings coming from God."

In an urban community many of the members of these lively Christian groups are houseservants who work under a strict regimen. They must do the laundry, the cleaning, the cooking, the washing up, but they must not talk. They definitely must not speak about their worries to their employers—it might be too embarrassing. For exactly the same reasons, they are not allowed to express themselves prayerfully in the official, traditional churches. There too it might cause embarrassment.

DIRECTNESS

A boy of about fourteen, an orphan who took care of six younger brothers and sisters on a small piece of land that had belonged to his father (a piece so small that nobody thought it worthwhile to chase him away from it), stood at the chapel door. He did not say anything. He handed me a letter. The letter was folded in such a way that it formed its own envelope. I opened it. It was a drawing. He had drawn an altar and on that altar a cross. Jesus hung nailed to that cross. I could see the four nails clearly. Some words were written as if coming out of the mouth of Jesus. The words were in hardly recognizable English: "Father Dadas pelece helpu mee" ("Father Donders, please, help you me"). Under the words a list of prices appeared. They had been added together: three parcels of maize meal at 3/60 each, one kilo of sugar 4/, and one pound of margarine 5/05. The total was 19/85, about $1.50.

That he asked for help was not so strange. The way in which he asked it must not have been strange to him either. He identified himself directly with the suffering Jesus on the cross. In the West one would call such an identification mystical if it were the case of a spiritual nun or monk. The boy had acted from his religious and human experience. The religious and profane were not separated in him. His religion had an immediate and direct effect on his life. Had he not been baptized? Had he not become an agemate of Jesus?

This direct relationship between the sacred and the profane is the reason that even the official churches have to take care of the "worldly" worries of their faithful. They have to. The Catholic Interdiocesan Secretariats and their corresponding National Councils of Christian Churches all have departments of health, education, social affairs, and agriculture. They would not be able to do without them. Those services are part of the worship of God.

26

Politics and the Christian Community

Some time ago the Organization of African Unity met in Nairobi. The heads of almost all the states in Africa came together for the meeting—about forty-two presidents, kings, and generals came. The whole town of Nairobi had been cleaned up. Beggars and prostitutes had been picked up and transported to far-off places. On the roads leading into town roadblocks were set up to prevent all suspicious (and shabbily dressed) people from entering town. The public buildings had been repainted; even the copper on the buildings had been polished. An old hotel that had been standing empty in the middle of town for several years waiting for the demolishers had been whitewashed. Nobody had any difficulties with all those measures. Everyone would have done the same at home in case of an important visitor.

There was one serious disappointment. The people in town acted as if nothing special was happening. No crowds lined the streets when the dignitaries were passing. Some school children waving little flags were there, but they had obviously been organized for the occasion. There was little public enthusiasm.

In one of the youth hostels a group of young African students from all over the continent watched the opening session over television. A clerk announced the participating presidents, kings, and generals one by one. It was an impressive list. After each announcement the heads of state applauded each other. The group of students remained silent. Then suddenly one of them said: "Crooks, they are all crooks!" There was no reaction. Nobody protested. Everyone seemed to agree. The remark deflated the whole political balloon in front of them. It *demythologized* that whole political show.

POSTPOLITICAL COMMUNITIES

To call political leaders crooks is new in Africa. One would not have said such a thing ten years ago. At that time everyone was caught up in the euphoria of newly won independence. Out of this euphoria the idea for the Organization of African Unity was born. At that time expectations were high. Every social problem, in fact every problem, was going to be solved. At that time people complained when church organizations wanted to do something for young, unemployed school dropouts, for the disabled or the sick. That should be done by the national government, they said. The government was going to solve all problems.

That type of remark is not made anymore and definitely not in the countries where there is much distress. The people do not hope anymore for effective government aid. Politics has become a few persons and personalities warring against each other, trying to profit as much from a situation as possible. It is not principles, plans, and policies.

The formation of numerous small Christian communities and the even more numerous independent church groups is to a great extent due to this crisis. Within the traditional African system, problems were solved within communities and by the formation or reorganization of those communities. The people know that the older communities do not work anymore. The communities are not capable of tackling modern problems because of the influence of urbanization.

Africans are trying to find new community forms. In regions with a strong Christian presence, that new community is often formed around Jesus. In regions with a strong Islamic presence, an Islamic community is often the new rallying point. African small Christian communities and independent churches are often compared with the Latin American basic communities.

Both these movements seem to be parallel in one way. They are both born in the context of a great distrust of the political structures in the two continents. That distrust led in Latin America to

Christian communities that politicized their members. In Africa the Christian communities do not politicize. They are trying to find apolitical survival in an over-politicized world. They are, so to speak, postpolitical, and they often say that of themselves.

POLITICS

It sounds fundamentalistic to call contemporary politics in general "devilish," not only at the level where the world powers are fighting for influence, but even at the level where separate countries have organized their national welfare systems. It has been said so often that it does not mean much anymore, but it is worth saying again: the spending of a million dollars a minute on armaments in the world is *demonic*, especially because the money is being spent in a world in which—because of the dangers and inequalities around us—few human beings can develop themselves freely.

Visitors from the West often say within a few days after their arrival in Africa, "The situation here is alarming. The difference between the rich and the poor is too great. It can't go on like this." They localize the problem in the so-called Third World. They speak about the misbehavior and the lack of responsibility of the leading classes in the Third World, but they forget that the poverty in an African (and Asian) slum and the hunger in the Sahel or in Bangladesh exist only about ten hours' flying time from their well-provided kitchens and dining rooms. (Much of the food in those Western kitchens and dining rooms even comes from those poor regions.)

The power of this world is divided over races, classes and special interest groups. For any one of those groups that holds power we could use the old Latin word *fascis*. The word referred to the bundle of sticks a Roman officer carried to indicate the number of men he commanded. This "fascist" organization of the world is the cause of its division, its armaments race. That division in its turn keeps the "fascist" organization of this world alive.

The linguist-philosopher Noam Chomsky, in a talk at the Polytechnic of Central London in 1981,[1] analyzed the world's political situation and explained that the leading politicians in the United States and the Soviet Union and their financial collaborators *need* the cold war to be able to keep their populations oppressed. He spoke of the possibility of a "counter-power," and said that more and more people in the world are no longer willing to accept their oppression. Even Christian leaders must know something about this possible "counter-power" because they declare that politics in this world cannot be based on the eight beatitudes. Since the eight beatitudes are the essence of the gospel, the whole of the gospel does not then seem to count in any "real" policy. There is probably more truth in this than even the politicians suppose. It is difficult to see how the eight beatitudes (and the petitions in the Our Father) are in line with what is happening politically in our world.

A reader of the Gospels would know that. Whatever exegetical explanation we accept, Luke makes a blunt remark on political power in the beginning of his Gospel. This remark must have corresponded to a Jewish or an early Christian intuition. When Satan had taken Jesus to the top of a mountain, from which he could see all the political kingdoms of the world, the devil told Jesus: "I will give you all this power and all this wealth. It has all been handed over to me, and I can give it to anyone I choose. All this will be yours, then, if you worship me." According to the text, and according to the intuition expressed in it, all political power and splendor was of the devil.

The text also gives us Jesus' reaction. He does not accept Satan's offer. He answers him with a quote from the Bible, one that he is going to fulfill later himself. He says: "Worship the Lord your God and serve him only." He revealed himself at that moment as the Word that, just as in the first story of Genesis, is sent into the world to order the chaos without becoming part of that chaos itself.

That story in Genesis received its final redaction during the Babylonian exile. It was probably edited then to give some comfort and consolation at a time when everyone had given up the hope of a restoration of the Jewish people. At that time, according to some exegetes, the Bible was not read as a history of salvation, but as the expression of God's will for a people in diaspora. In this reading the Bible gave the people a new identity.

It must have been from that inspiration or intuition that Jesus rode his donkey into Jerusalem in solemn entry. He did not even ride a fully grown donkey, but a colt. The prophet Zechariah had spoken about that donkey and its rider as someone who would ban all war chariots and tanks, all horses and missiles, one who would end war once and for all.

The empire that started from that donkey's back would cover the whole of the earth. All through the Gospels Jesus gives signs of counterpower; he compares his kingdom with a seed, with salt, light, yeast. The greatest sign he gave of that counterpower was when he, delivering his alternative lifestyle into the hand of the powers of his time, proved victorious over them by his resurrection. The Word, which he was and is, undid once and for all the chaos in this world. The new life was born, a new alternative. Humanity would no longer be divided into races, tribes, and classes. Human life itself would be the issue.

PRACTICAL POSSIBILITY

We can reasonably ask whether such an alternative as that offered by Jesus is not an impossibility. Indeed practicing politicians say that it is impossible. The Christian alternative must have looked absurd to the Roman powers of the first century. The Roman Empire had reached the zenith of its power. Within that empire the Christian minority, which sabotaged official power politics and hardly participated in public Roman life, was looked upon with disgust. The disciples of Jesus Christ were officially depicted as donkey-heads. Who could have suspected at that time what was going to happen? Who could have anticipated that only two centuries later Augustine would write off the whole mighty Roman empire in the name of Christianity?

We have witnessed in our own days the collapse of colonial power structures. What would the British proconsuls and viceroys, the Curzons and Cromers have said, in their heyday if someone had told them that their empire was soon going to end? In the town of New Delhi Sir William Lutyens designed a palace for the British viceroy that could function for centuries.

To ask whether the alternative is possible is not the right question. The African small Christian communities were started as the existing political and economic situation became impossible. Within those new communities they are trying to change the old power-complex into a new family-complex, the old money-economy into a new life-economy. The same movement is observable in America and in Europe. Maybe the day is not so far away when the Old Testament, the New Testament, the Islamic, the Taoist, and even the postreligious Marxist prophecies of a stateless world will be fulfilled. That world would be *a community of communities* in which no elite, neither priestly, political, nor economic, would exploit or deceive the others.

The need for such an alternative, postpolitical life-organization is not only to be found in religious circles. Humanity is being reorganized and reoriented throughout the world in many ways. William P. Reyburn pointed out in a talk at Driebergen, Holland, in 1972 that the number of languages officially recognized and spoken in Europe is increasing all the time.[2] According to his research, in 1800 only sixteen languages were officially recognized in Europe. In 1900 there were thirty (and the newly recognized languages were spoken by eighty million people). In 1937 fifty-three languages were recognized, and since then another four have been added to the number. Regionalism is growing at the same time as is a universalizing tendency. The League of Nations and the United Nations with their global programs not only universalize the care for environment, education, health, and habitat; they also sensitize all cultures by their proclamations of a year for the child, for women, for the disabled, refugees, the aged, and youth. Between these two developments—regionalism and universalism—the sovereign states seem to be losing their function.

In several African countries this has already happened. The only functioning communities are the religious ones, where people look for salvation and help from each other in an apolitical way. The power and might of these communities come from the man who entered Jerusalem triumphantly sitting upon a colt.

27

Politics and God

A coup had been attempted early in the morning. Members of the air force had stormed the local radio station shouting "Power!" People joining them in the streets shouted the same word. Passersby who did not even know English had to give the same greeting to the rebels and their sympathizers: "Power!" The rebellion was suppressed because other troops faithful to the ruling government were more powerful, with their guns and automatic rifles. They did not have to shout power; they had power.

The government ruled with that power. Under that power fewer and fewer people owned more and more land, houses, and other property. A few days before the attempted coup a student had shouted during a demonstration: "This country is the property of 10 percent of the population!" Someone else interrupted him: "That is not true; it is the property of 1 percent of the population."

Power and violence are the problems of our times. They are the problems of Africa. The Ghanaian scholar John S. Pobee's book *Toward an African Theology* contains a chapter on the topic "The Ethics of Power." Violence and power are problems not only because of their extent and potential. They are also problems because they seem rooted so deeply in us.

HYPOCRISY

The Sunday after the coup all the churches were full, whereas on the Sunday the coup took place almost nobody had gone to church. Pastors and faithful had heeded the warning of the rebels not to move through the streets. But a week later all was quiet again. God was thanked, jubilantly, for saving the ruling powers. An American pastor said enthusiastically in his televised sermon "Our God did not sleep. When the henchmen of Satan attacked, our God did not sleep; he guarded over his sons and daughters!" Did that preacher have any knowledge of the dangers American interests in the country would have faced if the coup had succeeded?

Next day the papers reported on some participants in an evangelization course that began on the day of the coup. Immediately after the news of the coup, they had started to pray, and Jesus had appeared to them assuring them that all would be well. The Catholic bishops bought a page in the local dailies to give warning that the "event" should be an invitation to all to examine their consciences. They even listed some of the points that should be considered, and they ended by saying that all authority comes from God. Someone asked a few days later in a letter to the editor whether the bishops would have said the same thing if the government had been overthrown, and whether that meant that they would have supported the new government. The people knew in their hearts that all church leaders probably would have done that. In that eventuality God would have been said to have helped the country to get rid of the leadership that was overthrown.

FORCEFUL DIVINITY

There is always a contradiction in the arguments and reflections on events that God is said to have helped. Someone heals because of God's intervention. If that is true, why did God not intervene before? God did not sleep, the preacher said, but if that is so, why did God not prevent the whole rebellion? At the local major seminary, directed by a Western staff, the professor of homiletics told his class that "God's Word has nothing to do with an event like a coup." He added: "The preacher is not supposed to give a running commentary on political events." The other extreme. Where is the balance found?

Isn't every theology a kind of anthropology? There is a good biblical reason to ask that question. According to the Bible we are created in God's image. There is consequently a relationship between the idea we have of ourselves and the idea we have of God. After having created an image of God that is pleasing to us, we have no difficulty imitating that God. When those of us who were brought up within the Judeo-Christian tradition consider God, we presuppose a belief in "creation." We have such self-assurance that we do not notice that this image of God as creator is a minority view even among those who believe in God or in a divinity. Most of humanity never thought of God as a creator. Chinese and Indian religions and philosophies use different images. Even our own Western ancestors never considered God in that way. There is not a trace of such belief in ancient Greek thought. We received the idea from the Judeo-Christian part of our heritage.

With the exception of a few isolated groups, Africans too consider God to be a creator. Experts discuss whether those Africans got this image of God from the Middle East or whether they exported the idea to the Middle East. Most scholars say the latter hypothesis seems unlikely. They seem to resist acknowledging the importance of African ideas. We still have to get accustomed to the idea that African (or "primary") religious thought might be of interest to the religious dialogue of the world. Even missionary societies that had great respect for the religious convictions of northern African Muslims rarely showed the same respect for the religious heritage of the sub-Saharan Africans.

The story of creation is a difficult story. Its difficulty has often been discussed. How can we speak about a beginning? Is God plus creation two? The pantheistic explanation of the genesis of the universe is simpler. The universe simply flows forth from God—a harmonious solution to the question of our origin.

Aside from these classical questions, others also can be asked. A creating God is a maker. Isn't every maker a force? Doesn't all making involve resistance? Isn't making always something of a conflictive situation? Isn't there always a difference between a subject and an object? Isn't there always in making a *one, two,* and *three*: thesis, antithesis, and synthesis? Another factor makes the creation story something "forceful": nature is "bent" according to God's ideas and words.

Ali Mazrui, a Kenyan, once told his students at the University of Nairobi: "Julius Nyerere is the most Western of all African leaders." When his amazed audience asked how he could say that, he answered: "He is constantly trying to impose his ideas on reality." This is characteristic of Western humanity and consequently of its God. Though both the Western and the African believer in God make God into a creator, the Western and the African interpretations of creation differ considerably. To put the whole story in a somewhat simplistic way: in both reports God blows life, breath, or spirit into an already formed body. In the Western version God makes that body from clay; in the African versions a lesser divinity often makes the body. But that is not the main difference between the two. After having received breath, in the Western interpretation, the human being begins, using that breath parcelled out to him or to her, an independent, individual life, though theoretically the theologians speak of "providence" and "sustainment." Human beings stand freely and independently in nature, which has been given to them as a life-space and especially as a work-space. (Our Western problem—imported to Africa—of unemployment has to do with this vision.)

The African interpretation (explained by theologians like Mulago and Sawyerr, and philosophers like Kagame and Hountoundji) sees the whole process differently. God continues to blow after the first breath has been received. Human life continues to be blown by God through the ancestors, forefathers and foremothers, grandparents and parents, of those who are now alive, and they in their turn make that life flow into their children. Besides, within the African framework, all other life—that of the minerals, the plants, and the animals—is given together with human life. Those manifestations of life were not meant for themselves, but for humanity.

MILD DIVINITY

The disadvantage of this African vision has nothing to do with the interpretation itself, but with the way in which it is often applied. Its application is usually restricted to one's own ethnic group, to one's own people. Although within those groups rituals and "safety valves" take care that peace and unity are maintained, the ethnic groups themselves are often bitter enemies. For example, some Masai are convinced that all cows were given to them by God almighty. If they see any cattle in the fields of others, they are convinced that they were once stolen from the Masai.

However, the African vision has a great advantage over other visions. It is a position between the Western *creation model* and the Asian belief in *emanation*. According to the Asian belief, all the universe is flowing forth from a supreme source, a divine principle. According to the African vision, the creation idea is combined with the notion of emanation. The African vision is a world vision, in which all is holy and, in a sense, even divine. Alien, forceful creative interference is softened by the "immanent" stream of life in everyone and everything. Creation is not over purposefully "directed."

We might compare the African vision with Alfred North Whitehead's process theology. Whitehead thought one of the advantages of his theology was that in it God interacted lovingly and mildly—not forcefully—with humanity and the world. The African vision of God was similar, but the Western image of God broke through this old and wise African image of God. The organic unity of life was interrupted with violence: "Power!" Power has always been used, in the West and elsewhere, in favor of some at the cost of others.

STABILITY

After the coup, peace returned. Letters from overseas mentioned again and again: "We hope that it is true that all unrest is over and that stability has been restored." Yes, all is quiet again. The tourists are returning. Investors are invited too. Everything is as it always has been. In almost every church God has been praised and thanked for that. Almost every preacher and spiritual leader has hastened to praise the renewed stability. The coup had been accompanied by several hours of lawlessness, confusion, looting, and killing—the law of the gun. And yet. . .

There is another aspect to the Western God as creator. Having given life, God leaves an established order. God thus becomes the guarantor of the existing order. The Swiss author Fritz Zorn wrote a book called *Mars* (War), shortly before he died of cancer.[1]

In that book he wrote that his sickness was due to the quiet and stability of his rich bourgeois family in Zurich. Theirs was the stability of the powerful, who isolate themselves in their name and in their riches. That unchanging milieu killed him, and he blamed God for his death. It was in the name of God, he argued, that his family frustrated and raped all humanity. Theirs was the stability of the powerful, who attribute their peace and welfare to God and isolate themselves in their wealth, leaving the rest of humankind to die in misery. Zorn (*Zorn* is one of the German words for anger) chose his pen name to show his wrath. He concluded that it might be better, perhaps, to ally oneself with God's opponent, Satan.

Was it not for a similar reason that the defenders of religious, civil, and political stability in Jerusalem considered Jesus to be possessed by Satan? Vincent Cosmao notes in his book *Changer le monde (Changing the World)* that when God is transformed into the guardian of law and order, atheism becomes a necessary condition for any social change.[2] Observing the world situation, who can escape the conviction that something, somewhere, went wrong? Don't many signs in the West point to an antiquated and unserviceable image of God (and consequently of ourselves)? Would not the African idea combining a belief in creation with a belief in emanation be a help?

28

Tinned Pineapple and Ecumenism

On a sunny afternoon in Thika some children were playing outside the town near the fenced-in pineapple plantations of the Del Monte Corporation. Some of the company guards did not trust the playful movements of the children. They let their dogs loose, and the animals attacked the children. One child was mauled to death, a second seriously injured. Both were taken to a hospital. That night a train left Thika for Mombasa, the most important harbor in East Africa. The train was loaded with tinned pineapples. One of the tinners was a parent of the child who had died.

The workers at the pineapple plant are paid badly for their work. Almost all are casual laborers. Thus the firm is not obliged to pay the (low) minimum salary, and it has no obligation to furnish benefits to their workers. In that industry, which is one of the most accident prone, the laborers earn an average of fifty to sixty dollars a month.

A few weeks after the incident described above, a birthday party was held somewhere in Europe. On the table was a huge fruit salad. Some tins from Kenya had been opened in the kitchen to prepare that salad. The guests said grace before eating: "Almighty Father, we thank you for the abundance of your gifts!" Everybody answered "Amen." The "Amen" was not heard in Thika.

CONTRADICTION

This type of story should be told often—not to spoil any celebration or feast, but to start a real ecumenical dialogue. Anyone hearing the above story knows that something is wrong. That knowledge should be the conscience of our age. Our conscience "speaks" when it observes a discrepancy between what we should do and what we actually do. As we steal, we know we should not. As we smoke, we know we should stop. This contradiction in us hurts us. If our conscience starts to prick as we hear the story from Thika, we are admitting to ourselves that what happened should not have happened. It was wrong. It is not difficult to find the origin of the discrepancy. Two factors are intermixed and contradict each other. A *conversion* should take place.

We are so well-organized in our world that we can eat each other's food even if the food is cultivated tens of thousands of miles away. We profit from labor in different parts of our world. At the same time, however, we are so divided and torn apart, that, without always knowing it, we are eating the food from each other's plates. It is our unity that has made our disunity possible.

FAILED ECUMENISM

Our story and others like it should start our real ecumenical dialogue. Anyone who has some knowledge of ecumenism knows that the idea is usually restricted to the Christian world, where different Christian communities oppose each other or are separated because of doctrinal or disciplinary differences. The churches' ecumenical activities try to overcome those difficulties and bring all churches together.

Up to now attempts to form one world-church have failed. Thank God! Just imagine if they had succeeded. Success would have meant, considering the reigning mentality in those churches and especially in church leadership, the formation of one gigantic powerbloc in the world. How would others, the non-Christians, have felt?

The failure to unite all the churches might be due to the too limited extent of ecumenical effort—too limited in the sense that the effort intends to "unite" Christians only and is geared primarily toward religious or denominational interests. Is the disappearance of the ecumenical enthusiasm of the 1950s and the 1960s not an indication of its quantitative and qualitative shortsightedness?

POWERBLOC

Though the establishment of a Christian world church failed, Christianity, nevertheless, forms, one bloc. Christianity was so long "on its own" in its expressions and forms that it organized itself independently of other human and cultural organizational forms. In its isolation it developed a life-pattern that simultaneously was determined by and influenced its historical situation. Christianity existed for too long within a closed circle. It became "christendom," a group, a phalanx, within the larger world. When they entered that larger world, Christians had become so accustomed to themselves and their own ways that anything else was strange, exotic, and wrong. Missionaries and evangelizers consequently tried to make all the "others" the same as themselves in prayer, work, life, marriage, health, and even death. Only very slowly did the strangeness of their behavior begin to dawn upon those apostolic workers in what they called "their" mission regions.

Gradually this insight took hold, and almost all of the missionaries now become interested in the cultures and religions of the people with whom they work. In many cases experienced missionaries even have decided to phase out their work in order to leave further developments to the autochthonous communities. Often they are asked to leave in view of a missionary moratorium.

While these representatives of the older, major missionary churches are leaving, paradoxically new missionaries are arriving. They are mostly members of fundamentalist groups, without any experience in the field. Older Protestant missionaries see themselves replaced by fundamentalist American evangelists; Catholic missionaries are often succeeded by Polish, Maltese, and American colleagues who often have no experience of other cultures and who are members of conservative, if not reactionary, communities.

REORIENTATION

Because of the growing insight into the value of other cultures and religious convictions, a reorientation of mission work seems to be demanded. We must find a new perspective and goal that will justify our mission endeavors. This justification should relate to today's world. If it does not, it will be ineffective. The new justification also should be based on fundamental Christian intuitions and beliefs. Unless it is, Jesus will disappear from our world.

In the process of formulating this justification a lot of traditionally ecclesial and theological deadwood will be cut away. Paul described his mission in his letter to the Ephesians as the revelation of a mystery, a secret that until the appearance of Jesus Christ had been hidden. The mystery or secret was that all human beings are *one*. All belong together in one. In his other letters Paul used the model of one body, of which Jesus is the head. John gives us Jesus' formulation of the same vision. Jesus calls himself the vine, and all human beings are the branches. Jesus tells the Samaritan woman that the moment of truth is near, and the truth is that all humanity has access to God.

In what many consider to be the earliest gospel text, Mark tells us that the officials decided to kill Jesus after he had stopped the selling in the temple after he had shouted: "My house shall be called a house of prayer for *all the nations*" (Mk. 11:17). When he was asked how we should pray, Jesus answered: "*Our* Father, *our* parent, *our* source," indicating not only how we should relate to God but also how we should relate to each other.

THE AFRICAN MODERN VISION

The growing feeling that we belong together is found not only in Western culture. In the midst of the frustrating national politics of many African countries, there is an extraordinarily strong will to break through tribal limitations in the direction of a larger community. The limitations of the tribal communities, which up to recently were the only valid and working possibilities for survival, caused many disappointments. Notwithstanding the potential dangers to their cultures, the will of Africans to change is tremendous.

They all want to be united with the rest of humanity. They hope to accomplish that through a community with all in Jesus Christ—the community Paul wrote about when he explained his mission. In such a community the whole of humanity would belong to one family, the family of God, in which all are brothers and sisters. This is the community prophesied by Isaiah and the other prophets, the community of which the people assembled in the streets of Jerusalem had a foretaste at Pentecost.

These ideas are not new to Africa. The ancient Egyptians had a symbol for the cosmos: an egg. Within an egg everything necessary to form the chicken is present. In the egg a chicken grows slowly under the influence of what the French physiologist Claude Bernard once called the *idée directrice*, the directive idea. Aren't we all—minerals, plants, animals, and human beings—in that cosmic egg, directed by an organizing principle that we call, in our belief and in our hope, the Holy Spirit?

Every tin filled with "exotic" fruits, every cup of coffee or tea, every bunch of bananas or grapes, should be seen in that *ecumenical* light. Didn't *oikoumene* originally mean *"the whole of the inhabited world"*? All those things that we use of each other's (often forced from the hands of those others) are signs of the conditions of today's world—signs of tragedy and signs of hope. Because of their hope in ecumenism Africans turn to Jesus, and through Jesus to us. They hope that we will turn to them, and to each other. Let us pray that their hope may not be in vain!

29

Born from the People of God

It is forbidden to add anything to or change a word of the four canonically fixed prayers of the Mass. Notwithstanding that prohibition priests do take liberties with the texts. The word *mine* is sometimes changed to *ours*. "Happy are those who are invited to your *supper*" is changed to "Happy are those who are called to your *banquet*." Those priests betray their feelings in these changes and their insights. For example, those who feel uneasy with all the references to the idea of sacrifice devise ingenious ways to avoid that word.

Other changes and amendments betray a lack of understanding and of insight. A text that is frequently amended, even in regions where one would usually expect faithfulness to the official texts, occurs after the consecration. The text reads: "Lord, remember your church throughout the world; make us grow in love, together with N. our pope, N. our bishop, and all the clergy." Many priests do not seem to be happy with that text, and they will add to it something like "and all your holy people." They are afraid that the people of God will not be mentioned. They do not realize that in praying for the church we are praying for the people. They do not see that in the text the people of God are mentioned first, "hoping that it will grow in love," with the pope, the bishops, and the clergy in a secondary place.

The church in Africa always has known itself to be the people of God. When the Second Vatican Council began to call the church "the people of God," this usage was hailed as a new development in ecclesiology by Western theologians like Yves Congar, Henri de Lubac, and Karl Rahner. To the African church the idea was not really new. The people never had known anything else in their experience.

Throughout this book most of the reasons for this belief have been mentioned. The church in Africa was brought, but neither planted nor built, by the clergy. All studies on the subject show that bishops and priests were only the coordinators of the work done by the lay people. The catechists, the teachers, the women did the real mission work. The bishops and priests never managed to bring the church institution and its hierarchy into the villages. The bishop never comes upcountry, and the priests only rarely come there.

The Christian community was a lay community from the very beginning. Most communities were, and still are, begun by lay people, not by the hierarchy. Their steady growth and the ever-decreasing number of priests have made the lay influence in the churches even greater. Activities formerly done by missionaries and religious more and more have been taken over by lay people. The Catholic church cannot work in the old, classical way. Activities once considered "clerical" are now performed by lay people with or without appropriate training.

This process has been strengthened by development among the religious, both African and expatriate. More and more congregations and societies are leaving their large houses and convents next to churches to go and live with the people, with the poor. Fewer religious are willing to work for the church as an institution, to fill holes and leaks in the established ecclesial organization. Many priests appointed to start a new town parish no longer begin by building a large church. In some cases they do not intend to ever construct such a church building. They consider their church to be the parishioners who have organized themselves into small groups and who in that way feel more united and close to each other and to Christ than they would have in the older setup.

FEARS

The members of small Christian communities do not come together for purely religious reasons, at least not in the Western sense. They do not only come together to assist at the Mass, to be blessed during benediction, or to say a rosary. They come together because they were used to overcoming their problems within a community where care for life and worship coincided.

Within an East African urban area the new Christian communities offer solidarity and security among people of different ethnic groups; upcountry they replace the traditional rural family pattern that is (unfortunately) rapidly falling apart.

The formation of these communities makes the hierarchy suspicious and afraid. It has difficulties with the growing influence of the lay people, who assume more and more of the power the bishops and priests formerly had (or thought they had) over the faithful. The hierarchy also fears the "secular" influence of these groups, especially when they speak out on issues of justice and peace. Many church leaders would like to change the order to peace and justice and in certain cases they have changed it.

The hierarchy in general is uneasy about the rising pressure from below, from the people, and thus it attempts to "domesticate" the people's religious inspirations and intuitions. The existing church leadership is trying hard to get all religious experience contained in nice, reassuring, censoring, and controlling legal forms. Instead of favoring spontaneous prayer, the saying of the rosary is encouraged; instead of allowing locally composed liturgies, a missal is imposed; instead of a communal tackling of injustice and sin, private confession is stressed; instead of the narratives of the Bible, the theology of the catechism is taught; instead of allowing lay-awareness programs to develop, the bureaucratic approach from above is preferred. As the church leadership tries to manipulate the religious experience of the faithful, believers disappear from the churches. They go underground insofar as they do not wish to belong to the "official" church anymore. The formation of every independent church is due to a misunderstanding, a failed power play, unfulfilled expectations, or the manipulation (and sometimes exploitation) of the good faith of the believers.

These happenings help us to understand what is going on not only in Africa but also in other continents. In the mirror of Africa we can better understand our own society and culture. Many processes and developments are hidden to the participant-observer in any human community. Familiarity with one's own society is not a blessing when one is faced with the task of describing or analyzing one's own experience. The fish notice the water last. As Wittgenstein once pointed out: "The aspects of things that are most important for us are hidden because of their simplicity and familiarity. (One is unable to notice something because it is always before one's eyes.)"[1]

It is customary in church circles to attribute the disappearance of practicing Christians from the churches in the West to the growing secularization of that society. The people who leave are at fault. The amazing thing is that whenever the religiosity of those who leave is checked and explored, the most astounding vein of religiosity is discovered. In 1982 when the Gallup Research Institute asked 20,000 Europeans from fifteen countries whether they believed in God, 75 percent answered in the affirmative; but when they were asked whether the churches satisfied their religious needs only about 36 percent answered yes.

Have Western church authorities and their theologians ever tried to find out what had meaning for their faithful? Is it any wonder that the faithful moved away from a church that was not interested in them, that checked only from time to time to see whether the flock was still orthodox in its beliefs, that is to say, believing what the church leaders believed?

When a church does not live the religious experience of its people, it is not a church anymore, notwithstanding all its learnedness, its culture, its liturgical splendor, and its defense of rich sponsors and the status quo. It becomes a skeleton. The live people move elsewhere. In East Africa they moved sometimes under the trees in front of the church building they left, giving new hope to those still inside.

FORMAL AFRICAN CHRISTIAN THEOLOGY

I have tried in this book to show the unique religious and theological developments taking place in a large part of Africa. One of the most serious objections against such a survey is its tendency to generalize. How is it possible to write an accurate report considering the variety of languages and cultures of such a vast area?

African specialists agree, however, that the nature of the hu-

man experience over the whole of sub-Saharan Africa is in general
the same. That experience is unique in the world. Its main com-
ponents are : (1) the African traditional religious experience;
(2) Christian information about Jesus, brought from the col-
onializing Western world; and (3) the actual social, political, and
economic situation of Africa in the world today. These compo-
nents have led to different types of religious practice and to different types of theology. The more extreme types of theology,
involving an element of escapism, do not take all three compo-
nents into consideration. On the one hand there is the attempt
to return to "the belief of our ancestors," (taking into account
only the first component); on the other hand there are the
fundamentalist—often Baptist—and classical—hierarchical Roman Catholic—forms of Christianity (taking only the second
component into account).

Between these extremes are the trends that try to combine the
first and second factors. The older form of this trend was a kind
of adaptation theology, sometimes called assimilation theology.
During the 1974 synod held in Rome, the theme of which was
"Evangelization," the bishops of Africa distanced themselves
from this type of theology and opted for the theology of incarnation. The relevant section of their declaration reads as follows:

> Our theological thinking must remain faithful to the
> authentic tradition of the church and, at the same time, be
> attentive to the life of our communities and respectful of
> our traditions and languages, that is, of our philosophy of
> life.
>
> Following this idea of mission, the bishops of Africa and
> Madagascar consider as being completely out-of-date the
> so-called theology of adaptation. In its stead, they adopt the
> theology of incarnation. The young churches of Africa and
> Madagascar cannot refuse to face up to this basic demand.
> They accept the fact of theological pluralism within the uni-
> ty of faith, and consequently they must encourage, by all
> means, African theological research. Theology must be
> open to the aspiration of the people of Africa if it is to help
> Christianity to become incarnate in the life of the peoples of
> the African continent. To achieve this, the young churches
> of Africa and Madagascar must take over more and more

responsibility for their own evangelization and total development. They must combine creativity with dynamic responsibility.[2]

Though they insisted that "theology must be open to the aspiration of the people of Africa," the bishops did not seem to arrive at more than a combination of factors (1) and (2). Six days later Pope Paul VI, worried about the declaration, warned that "it would nevertheless be dangerous to speak of diversified theologies according to continents and cultures." He widened the discussion by saying: "Thus we consider necessary a word on the need of finding a better expression of faith to correspond to the racial, social, and cultural milieu."[3] He seemed to invite theologians to take factor (3) into consideration too.

The whole of the African experience seems to be reflected upon only by the group called the African Third World Theologians. Their theology began embryonically in southern Africa in some independent churches before the countries of that region attained independence. This theology is based on themes that directly refer to the mission of Moses at the court of Pharaoh. This form of liberation theology is sometimes compared to American black theology. There are some similarities, one of which is "the attempt of both African and American theology to rip off the foreign swaddling clothes and thus to expose the authentic, naked kerygma."[4] A key difference between the two theologies has to do with the fact that they are engaged with dissimilar cultures.

A similar difference exists between the African liberation theologies in southern Africa and an Africa Third World theology for which there is growing interest in the rest of Africa. Another problem and cause of divisiveness within African theology is that African theologians, notwithstanding their intentions to study and represent the contemporary African religious experience, often belong to the formal theological world of their Western colleagues.

HOPE

It is sometimes said that what we consider non-Western nowadays once was Western. The African, or primary, human experience is for that reason much nearer to the Western heart and mind than we first supposed it to be. We know that gradually in our Western world our hearts and minds have become alienated from us. This alienation is a recurring theme in Western literature, art, science fiction, and philosophy. Maybe we will find again, in what has become alien to us, something of ourselves, to the salvation of all of us.

Notes

INTRODUCTION

1. Walbert Bühlmann, *The Coming of the Third Church* (1978); *The Missions on Trial* (1979); *All Have the Same God* (1980); *The Chosen Peoples* (1982)—all published by Orbis Books.
2. The original was written in Dutch: *Bantoe filosofie* (Antwerp: De Sikkel, 1943). An English translation, *Bantu Philosophy*, was published by Présence Africaine (Paris, 1959).
3. Alexis Kagame, *La Philosophie bantoue-rwandaise de l'être* (Brussels: Académie Royale Scientifique Coloniale, 1956).
4. Henri Maurier, *Philosophie de l'afrique noire* (Bonn: Anthropos, 1976), pp. 36, 47.
5. Karol Wojtyla, *The Acting Person*, trans. Andrzej Potocki (Hingham, Mass.: Kluwer Boston, Reidel, Dordrecht, 1979).
6. Ibid., p. 299.
7. Daughters of St. Paul, comp., *John Paul II: Africa Apostolic Pilgrimage* (Boston: St. Paul's Editions, 1980), pp. 200–201.
8. Ibid., p. 216.
9. John S. Pobee, *Toward an African Theology* (Nashville, Tenn.: Abingdon Press, 1979), p. 49.

1   THE EXTENDED AFRICAN GOD-EXPERIENCE

1. See E. W. Fashole-Luke, ed., *Christianity in Independent Africa* (London: Rex Collings, 1978).
2. See Kofi Appiah-Kubi and Sergio Torres, eds., *African Theology en Route* (Maryknoll, N.Y.: Orbis Books, 1978), p. 64.
3. Ibid., p. 60.
4. The incidents were recounted by A. B. T. Byaruhanga-Akiiki in his paper "The Philosophy of Cursing" delivered at the Pan-African Philosophical Conference on Development, Ideology, Religion, and Philosophy, held in Khartoum, 1977.
5. See Harry Sawyerr, *God, Ancestor or Creator* (Bristol: Western Printing Services, 1968).

2 GOD AS A MEMBER OF THE HUMAN FAMILY

1. Harry Sawyerr, *Creative Evangelism* (London: Lutterworth Press, 1968).
2. Jomo Kenyatta, *Facing Mount Kenya* (London: Secker and Warburg, 1938).
3. Shiva Naipaul, *North of South* (London: Deutsch, 1978).
4. David Barrett, *Schism and Renewal in Africa: An Analysis of Six Thousand Religious Movements* (Nairobi: Oxford University Press, 1968).
5. Teresia Hinga, *An African Understanding of Salvation: The Case of the Ahonoki in Kiambu District* (Nairobi: University of Nairobi, 1980).
6. See Brian Hearne, "Basic Christian Communities," in Padraig Flanagan, ed., *A New Missionary Era* (Maryknoll, N.Y.: Orbis Books, 1982), pp. 92–98.
7. See Raphael Ndingi, "Basic Communities: The African Experience," in Flanagan, ed., *A New Missionary Era*, pp. 99–106.

3 LITURGY AS A FAMILY FEAST

1. *African Ecclesial Review* 20 (June 1978): 182–84.
2. See Sawyerr, *Creative Evangelism*.

4 GOD'S FAMILY

1. Gabriel M. Setiloane, "Where Are We in African Theology?" in Appiah-Kubi and Torres, eds., *African Theology*, p. 66.
2. John S. Mbiti, *African Religions and Philosophy* (Nairobi: Heinemann, 1969), pp. 97–99.
3. Ndingi, "Basic Communities," p. 101.

5 WHEN HUMAN LIFE IS THE MAIN ISSUE

1. Eugene Hillman, *Polygamy Reconsidered* (Maryknoll, N.Y.: Orbis Books, 1975).
2. Augustine, *Contra Faustum Manichaeum*, lib. xxii, c. 47, in P.L. 42, col. 428. English translation from *A Selected Library of Nicene and Post-Nicene Fathers of the Christian Church*, ed., Philip Schaff, et al. (Grand Rapids, Mich.: William B. Eerdmans, 1956), IV, p. 289.
3. Aylward Shorter and Benezei Kisembo, eds., *African Christian Marriage* (London: Chapman, 1977).
4. Hillman, *Polygamy*, p. 12.

6   BEGINNING ONLY

1. Malcolm McVeigh, *God in Africa* (Cape Cod: Hartford Stark, 1974).
2. Ibid., pp. 152-53.
3. Ibid., p. 153.
4. Efraim Anderson, *Church at the Grass Roots* (New York: Friendship Press, 1968), p. 149.
5. McVeigh, *God in Africa*, p. 180.

7   PAST AND FUTURE NOW

1. Kwasi Wiredu, "Morality and Religion in Akan Thought," in H. Odera Oruka and D. A. Masolo, eds., *Philosophy and Cultures: Proceedings of the Second Afro-Asian Philosophy Conference,* (Nairobi: Bookwise Ltd., 1983).
2. Martin Heidegger, *Sein und Zeit*, 9th ed. (Tübingen: Niemeyer, 1960), p. 286. English translation: *Being and Time*, trans. John Macquarrie and Edward Robinson (New York: Harper and Row, 1962), p. 332. Cf. José P. Miranda, *Being and the Messiah* (Maryknoll, N.Y.: Orbis Books, 1977), pp. 18-19.
3. John S. Mbiti, *New Testament Eschatology in an African Background* (London: Oxford University Press, 1971), p. 24.

8   TERRORIZED BY THE WRITTEN WORD

1. René Bureau, *Péril blanc: Propos d'un ethnologie sur l'Occident* (Paris: Editions Harmattan, 1978).
2. Desmond Tutu, "Black Theology/ African Theology: Soul Mates or Antagonists?", in Gayraud S. Wilmore and James H. Cone, eds., *Black Theology: A Documentary History, 1966-1979* (Maryknoll, N.Y.: Orbis Books, 1979), p. 490.

10   COMMUNITY POWER AND INSTITUTIONAL IMPOTENCE

1. *The Catholic Worker* 45 (June 1979).

11   THE YEAR OF THE JUBILEE

1. Harold Miller, "Jubilee 1981 among the Gabbra," *African Ecclesial Review* 23, no. 6 (Dec. 1981): 353-58.

13   THE PEOPLE'S PRIEST

1. See Brian Hearne, "Priestly Ministry and Christian Community," *African Ecclesial Review* 24, no. 4 (April 1982), pp. 221–34.
2. Ibid., p. 232.
3. Ibid., p. 223.

14   SPIRITUAL IMPERIALISM

1. Philip Potter, *De Tijd,* (Sept. 1980).
2. Eugene Hillman, *The Roman Catholic Apostolate to Nomadic Peoples in Kenya: An Examination and Evaluation* (Brussels: Pro Mundi Vita, 1980).
3. Joseph C. Pearce, *The Crack in the Cosmic Egg* (New York: Simon and Schuster, 1971).

15   FORGIVENESS AND COMMUNITY

1. Vincent J. Donovan, *Christianity Rediscovered* (Maryknoll, N.Y.: Orbis Books, 1982).
2. Lambert Bartels, "Reconciliation and Penance: A View from Ethiopia," *African Ecclesial Review* 25, no. 4 (August 1983), pp. 220–26.

16   SO MANY MYTHS

1. Placide Tempels, *Bantu Philosophy* (Paris: Présence Africaine, 1959), p. 17.
2. Ibid.

17   DENOMINATIONALISM AND RELIGION

1. John S. Mbiti, *African Religions and Philosophy* (New York: Doubleday, 1970).

19   WITHOUT FATHER

1. Kenneth Little, *African Women in Town: An Aspect of Africa's Social Revolution* (New York: Cambridge University Press, 1973).
2. Elizabeth Colson, "Family Change in Contemporary Africa," in John Middleton, ed., *Black Africa: Its People and Its Culture Today* (New York: Macmillan, 1970).
3. *The Synod on the Family: The Contribution of the Local Churches* (New York: Prospective International, 1981), p. 8.

4. Ibid., p. 9.

5. Philip Mbithi, *The Actual Situation of the Family in East Africa* (Nairobi: University of Nairobi, 1981).

20 SCIENCE AND RELIGION

1. Walbert Bühlmann, *The Missions on Trial*, trans. A. P. Dolan (Maryknoll, N.Y.: Orbis Books, 1979).

2. See P. Feyerabend, *Against Method* (London: NLB, 1975), p. 50.

3. O. M. de Vaal, *Modern medisch advies* (Amsterdam: Querido, 1967), p. 213.

4. Robin Horton, "African Traditional Thought and Science," *Africa* 37 (1967), 87–155.

5. William James, *The Varieties of Religious Experience* (New York: The New American Library, 1958), p. 378.

6. Ibid., p. 105.

22 PAIN AND SUFFERING

1. Okot P. Bitek, *Africa's Cultural Revolution* (Nairobi: Macmillan, 1973), p. 88.

2. Ibid.

3. *Religious Experience in Humanity's Relation with Nature: A Consultation, Yaounde 1978* (Geneva: World Council of Churches, 1979).

4. *The Witness of Edith Barfoot* (Oxford: Blackwell, 1977).

23 NON-BOURGEOIS THEOLOGY

1. Bernard Delfgaauw, *A Concise History of Philosophy* (Dublin: Gill and Macmillan, 1968).

2. Paulin J. Hountoundji, *African Philosophy, Myth and Reality*, trans. Henri Evans with Jonathan Rée (Bloomington: Indiana University Press, 1983).

3. Evan M. Zuesse, *Ritual Cosmos: The Sanctification of Life in African Religions* (Athens, Ohio: Ohio University Press, 1980).

4. Ibid., p. 3.

5. H. J. Becken, "Woder Glaube noch jung ist," *Neue Zeitschrift für Missionwissenschaft* 36, no. 1 (1981): 1–15.

24 WORSHIPPING DEVELOPMENT

1. *Major Evaluation of the Development Education Programme in Kenya 1974-1981* (Nairobi: Christian Development Education Service, 1983).

2. Quoted in Philip Scharper and John Eagleson, eds., *The Radical Bible* (Maryknoll, N.Y.: Orbis Books, 1972), p. 13.

3. Ibid.

25 PRAYER AS POWER

1. Faith Annette Sand, "No More Foreign Missions?" *National Catholic Reporter* 19, no. 34 (July 1, 1983): 18.

26 POLITICS AND THE CHRISTIAN COMMUNITY

1. *The Guardian Weekly* 124, 25 (June 21, 1981): 8–9.
2. William D. Reyburn, "Secular Culture, Missions, and Spiritual Values," in Matthew Black and William A. Smalley, eds., *On Language, Culture and Religion: In Honor of Eugene A. Nida* (The Hague: Mouton, 1974), pp. 287–99.

27 POLITICS AND GOD

1. Fritz Zorn, *Mars* (London: Pan Books, 1982).
2. Vincent Cosmao, *Changer le monde* (Paris: Cerf, 1979), p. 146; Eng. trans., *Changing the World* (Maryknoll, N.Y.: Orbis Books, 1984), p. 84.

29 BORN FROM THE PEOPLE OF GOD

1. Ludwig Wittgenstein, *Philosophical Investigations*, 3d. ed. (Oxford: Blackwell, 1968), no. 129.
2. "Synod Bishops from Africa Issue Declaration," *AMECEA Documentation Service* (Nairobi) 11 (1972): 2–3.
3. *Holy Father's Address at Conclusion of Synod of Bishops, 26 October 1974, L'Osservatore Romano* 45 (3435) (Nov. 7, 1974), p. 9.
4. Gabriel M. Setiloane, "About Black Theology," in *WSCF: A New Look at Christianity in Africa* 2, no. 2 (Geneva, 1972): 65–71.